THE AGE OF CHIVALRY

PART 2

Other volumes of The Age of Chivalry

Part 1 – The 8th to the 15th century

Helmets and mail

Tournaments and heraldic bearings

Bows and crossbows

Part 3 – The Renaissance

Arms, horses and tournaments

Helmets and armour

Tactics and artillery

THE AGE OF CHIVALRY

PART 2
Castles, forts and artillery,
8th to 15th century; Armour,
12th to 15th century; Infantry
of the Renaissance; Cavalry of
the Renaissance; The Slavs
and Orientals to the end of
the Renaissance

Liliane and Fred Funcken

Prentice-Hall, Inc., Englewood Cliffs, N.J.

First published in Great Britain in 1981
by Ward Lock Limited, London, a Pentos
Company.

First American edition published by
Prentice-Hall, Inc., 1983.

Printed and bound in Belgium by
Casterman S.A., Tournai

ISBN 0 − 13 − 046292 − 6 (Paper)
      0 − 13 − 046318 − 3 (Cloth)

Contents

I CASTLES AND ARTILLERY

The castle

The castle first appeared in the 10th century, at the dawn of the age of feudalism, in the form of a wooden tower called the keep which was built on either a natural or an artificial mound known as a motte. In fact the original word for 'keep' (*dunio, dunjonem, domgionem* in old texts, and *donjon* in modern French) originally meant the mound on which the tower was built.

Keeps such as this literally mushroomed, and any leader who had a certain amount of power lost no time in erecting one – sometimes so close to his neighbour that he could exchange arrow fire with him whenever a conflict flared up. Moreover ownership of such a 'castle' (from the Latin *castrum, castellum*) meant the creation of a seigniory.

We are reminded of how numerous these early motte and bailey keeps were by the toponymy, or place-names, of certain regions; in France, for example, where the word for mound was also 'motte', names such as La Motte, La Motte-Beuvron, La Motte-Feuilly, etc., are quite common.

These castles, which were veritable dens, all had without exception one special feature: there was no door on the ground floor. Entry into the castle was always gained via an opening at first floor level, to which access was provided by a ladder or a light, temporary footbridge; this could be withdrawn after use, thereby preventing any possibility of a surprise attack.

Most of these wooden towers were surrounded by a stockade, and here, too, traces of the past can be found in surviving place-names; for example the French words 'plessis' and 'haie', meaning 'enclosure', occur in names of towns such as Le Plessis-Bourré and La Haye-Descartes. The largest fortifications had a long footbridge which rested on fragile

THE DEVELOPMENT OF THE CASTLE

1. Early castle (9th to 10th century). We have no clear idea of what these towers looked like. They were usually built to a quadrangular plan, as this was the shape best suited to wooden buildings. In France, fortresses like these literally mushroomed up to the end of the 9th century, when legislation was introduced to regulate the number of them. 1a. Early keep as envisaged by Viollet-le-Duc. This 'pagoda' has been the subject of much debate and criticism, though no-one as yet has succeeded in coming up with a better idea. 1b. Blockhouse dating from the American colonial era with an overhanging storey for the defence of the walls and door. It would surely not be making too many assumptions to credit the Normans with an equal amount of ingenuity when they colonized England. 2. 11th-century Norman castle. The overall plan of the building varied depending on the lie of the terrain and the wealth of the seigneur. The basic outline could either be in the shape of a square or a more or less elongated rectangle. The natural or man-made mound or motte on which the keep was sited was usually 10 to 12 metres in height, though it could be as high as 35 metres, as in the case of the motte at Thetford in Norfolk. There must have been a transitional period between the decline of the wooden keep and the advent of the stone keep during which both timber and masonry were used, as above. The footbridge (a) had transverse bars which meant that the horses could be led inside the keep in times of extreme danger; once they were all safely inside the flimsy footbridge was destroyed. 3. Low-built stone keep (10th century). This type of building replaced the wooden keep when there was a natural as opposed to a man-made motte. An artificial motte could not have supported the weight of a stone keep. 4. Anglo-Norman castle (late 11th century). From the following century onwards the corner towers, and eventually the keep itself, were built to a circular ground plan so as to be less vulnerable to sapping. 5. The Castle of Coucy, in the department of the Aisne, in France, remains unrivalled in the field of military architecture. It was built between 1225 and 1230 and the towers were part of the original castle built by the ambitious Enguerrand III. The towers were 36 metres high and 18–19 metres in diameter, or, to put it another way, bigger than any of the king's own keeps, with the exception of the

1a

1b

1

a

2

3

4

5

L. & J. Funcken

tower of the Louvre which was 20 metres high. The colossal keep rose to 54 metres in height and had a diameter of 31 metres. Everything in this fortress was built to a huge scale: the staircases, the benches and the battlements all seem to have been designed for men of above-average height. After surviving a first attempt to demolish it under Cardinal Mazarin in the 17th century, the keep and the towers were finally dynamited by the German army in 1917. Today all that remains of the most remarkable castle in Europe are some nondescript ruins.

THE CASTLE AND ITS VARIOUS PARTS

1. Gatehouse or bastille. When this structure was temporary it was called a bastide. 2. Palisade made of wooden stakes, with gate. 3. Enclosed area, or bailey. 4. Barbican. 5. Crenellated ramp. 6. Main entrance. 7. Drawbridge and portcullis. 8. Breteche. 9. Sockets into which hoarding (see fig. 13) could be fitted. 10. Loopholes or arrow-slits. 11. Crenel or rectangular slit made in the parapet. 12. The merlon, or the part of the parapet between two crenels. (The merlon is often wrongly taken to mean the actual slit itself.) 13. Wooden hoards or hoarding, which were used until the 15th century. 14. Watch-tower or echaugette. 15. Curtain wall, or continuous fortifying wall. 16. These small galleries, which nowadays are often taken for breteches, were in fact merely common-or-garden latrines. 17. Postern with a ramp by which supplies were allowed into the castle. Some great castles, like Pierrefonds, for example, took in fresh provisions by this route so as to avoid any likelihood of a surprise attack or the possible entry of a spy into the building. Heavy loads and any livestock that was slaughtered outside the confines of the castle were hauled up the central slide of the ramp by a windlass. 18. Beak or spur tower. 19. Machicolation. 20. Shutters. As well as providing protection they also screened the

archer or crossbowman from the glare of the sun and prevented him from being seen by the enemy; he was thus able to take aim at his leisure. Note the stone hoarding, which gradually came to replace wooden hoards in the course of the 14th century. 21. Main buildings and living quarters. 22. Keep. Its machicolations (19) are concealed beneath arches which are supported by buttresses. 23. Look-out tower. 24. Tower built so as to be 'open at the throat', that is, completely open at the side facing inwards towards the keep. This meant that if the enemy succeeded in taking the tower they would find themselves exposed to fire from the garrison. 25. Weather-cocks. The weather-cock was a seigneurial prerogative which could be painted or cut to the shape of the owner's armorial bearings and used as an ensign. 26. Flanking tower.

KEEPS

1. 11th century Norman keep, 28 metres high and 16 metres across: A. The storeroom, well and staircase. The spiral staircase ascended in a clockwise direction; this meant that an invader had to climb the steps at the same time as fighting off the defender with the central pillar on his right. As a result his freedom of movement to use his weapons was greatly restricted, whereas the defender found himself in the opposite and far more advantageous situation of being shielded on his left-hand side by the pillar and having room on his right hand to wield his sword. Any reader who is interested can try this out next time he visits a castle and see for himself how amazingly effective this simple arrangement is. B. Chapel and guardhouse. C. The great hall. D. Sleeping quarters. E. Partition wall enabling a last attempt at resistance to be made if besieging troops succeed in penetrating into one or other part of the keep. 2. Round keep (early 13th century), 14 metres in diameter and 45 metres high: A. Living quarters of the seigneur and his family. B. Defence level. C. Cross-section of

the chemin de ronde and its hoarding (D). 3. Keep of the Castle of Coucy (early 13th century), 31 metres in diameter and 54 metres high: A. Ground-floor: storeroom for provisions and weapons. B. 1st floor: the seigneur's apartments. C. 2nd floor: living quarters of the garrison, which could take up to 1,000 men. D. 3rd storey: this was the defence level and was open to the sky. E. Opening of the shaft via which munitions stored on the ground floor were brought up. F. Hoards built on two levels (see special plate). 4. Construction of the keep at the Castle of Coucy and its ingenious spiral ramp. The ramp meant that the laborious business of hauling war engines up by hand could be avoided. The dotted red line indicates the level of the ground floor. 4a. Detailed view showing the spiral sockets for the ramp with a truss and guardrail. The keep of the Norman seigneur shown in fig. 1 was more like the den of a wild animal than a building in comparison with the keep in fig. 3; the latter is more systematically thought out, and every last detail is planned and worked out. And yet it was in the dark, cramped quarters of the 11th-century keep (which today would not even be fit for a prison) that the feudal lord acquired the arrogant self-confidence of the master who knew himself to be impregnable in his own stronghold; at the same time he developed a strong attachment to the idea of the family and the traditions and moeurs of his caste. In France it took the revolution of 1789 to wrest from the nobility the last of their remaining exorbitant privileges. Figs. 1, 2 and 3 are drawn to the same scale so as to give a more accurate impression of the relative size of the keep of Enguerrand III.

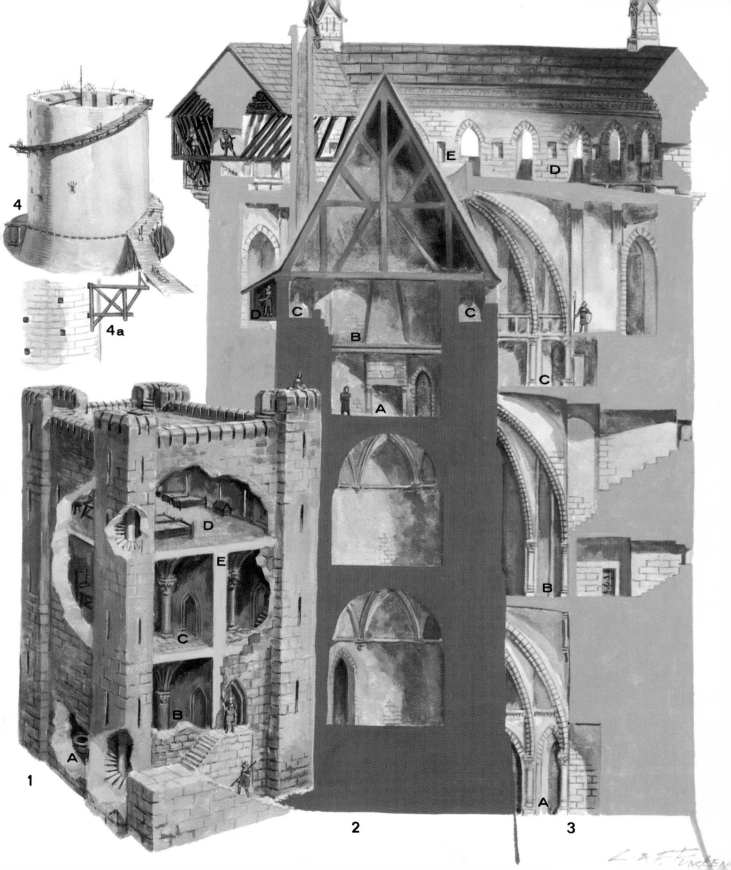

4

4a

1

2

3

D

C

B

A

E

C

B

A

D

C

B

A

C

E

D

A

B

supports; this footbridge started from the outside terreplein (which was surrounded by a stockade) and sloped gently up towards the raised area outside the door of the keep, thereby commanding a view of the entire fortified perimeter.

The 12th-century chronicler Jean de Colmieu, who was the biographer of Jean de Warneton, bishop of Thérouanne, recounted the unfortunate experience that befell the bishop when he visited the castle of Merchem, on the way to his diocese. Having stepped onto the precarious footbridge with too many other people, the rash prelate and his retinue found themselves in a heap in the moat, 10 metres below! A bridge of this height was not unusual, as a moat 35 metres above ground-level has been measured at Thetford in Norfolk.

The power of the nobles was, of course, measured by the size of their fortress, and it was they who built most of the early stone keeps, at the same time frequently forbidding their vassals to follow their example so that in the event of revolt they would have little difficulty in destroying any rebel hideout.

Suger, the abbot of Saint-Denis, has provided us with an excellent illustration of the speed with which wooden castles were erected and demolished in his *Life of Louis VI* (known as 'The Fat'). In 1111, this monarch decided to lay siege to the castle of Le Puiset in the Beauce, whose owner, Hugues du Puiset, had for some years been extorting dues from the local populace.

The king's army found a keep covered with the hides of newly-flayed animals that looked like a butcher's stall or a shop belonging to a dealer in animal skins.[1] During the first assault on the castle the villeins of the parish militias sustained terrible losses. The besiegers were on the point of beating a sorry retreat when an old priest rushed forward and, taking advantage of an angle where he was out of range of the defenders' missiles, uprooted a few of the stakes in the stockade. The breach was widened by the priest's flock, and the way opened for a flood of royal troops to enter. Hugues du Puiset was finally brought to bay at the top of his overrun keep; after his surrender his lair was set on fire.

After being sent into exile, the robber-baron made such a show of repentance that the good-natured Louis VI pardoned him. Immediately the incorrigible marauder rebuilt his keep

[1] See p. 28, Sieges (iii), fig. 2.

14

DEFENSIVE WORKS

1. Great drawbridge for horses and carts with the postern drawbridge for pedestrians adjacent to it. 1a. Detail of the counter-balancing mechanism. 2: a) drawbridge; b) mechanism for raising the drawbridge with its winch and counterweight; c) portcullis; d) mechanism for raising the portcullis (see fig. 4); e) exit postern and its hand-operated bascule bridges. The ground leading to the entrance of many fortresses tends to slope fairly steeply – as the weary tourist of today knows to his cost. This slope was intended to check the progress of an assailant while correspondingly increasing the force of any counter-attack. 3. Bascule bridge constructed without chains so as to forestall any possibility of damage by artillery fire. The arrows indicate how the bridge is operated by the winch, which lies in the shelter of the wall and is thus protected from possible damage. 4. Mechanism of a portcullis: a) bars for locking the lowered portcullis in position; these were secured by means of metal pegs sunk in the wall; b) and c) the portcullis was raised by disengaging the bars and fastening them to the links of the side chains (b) with hooks (c). 5. Classic type of drawbridge (14th century). These bridges were considered something of a risk when they provided access to a walled town, as there was always the danger of betrayal from within. For this reason whenever a town came under siege the gates defending the drawbridge were immediately walled up. 6. Loop-hole for firearms with machicolation (15th century). 6a. Cross-section of the same loop-hole. 7. Shuttered battlements and machicolation built in the form of a watchtower (13th century). 7a. Cross-section of the machicolation and quatrefoil loop-hole. 8. When side partitions were added, the shutter or mantlet (fig. 7) became a hutch, or *huchette*. 9. Various types of arrow-slit. The cruciform shape originally dated from the 14th century, but became more widespread in the 15th. On the right is a sectional view of the various kinds of arrow fire: a) firing at maximum elevation and range; b) firing straight ahead at medium range; c) firing at point-blank range. In addition the horizontal bar of the cross allowed the direct firing range to be extended a short distance to the right and left. In the 15th century the wide arrow-slits that had tended to weaken walls disappeared from use; previously a sapper had only to dig out a space between two loop-holes for the entire section of intervening wall to collapse. From that time onwards it

1 1a 4 2 b c d a e 3 5 6 6a 7 7a 8 9 a b c 10 11 a a 12

L. & F. Funcken

and started on his old tricks again. This gave rise to another campaign against him, which ended, like the first, with the burning of his keep. Punished and pardoned yet again, Hugues went on to rebuild his keep for a third time. This was the last straw. A third fire rid the Beauce once and for all of its obstinate oppressor.[1]

Reading this, it is easier to understand how William the Conqueror and his followers could occupy England simply by building keeps all over the country and then establishing themselves in them in the midst of a hostile populace. A century later, in the reign of Henry II, their descendants (who were now Anglo-Normans) used a similar method to subjugate Ireland.

Wooden constructions remained in use for a long time despite the ever-present risk of fire. Richard the Lionheart,[2] King John Lackland[3] and many other great lords built fortifications of which the *turres ligneae* were still an important feature. In 1301, when the ramparts of Bruges were dismantled by the French, they were still found to contain many sections made of wood. Camille Enlart has shown how certain types of fortification continued to use timber in conjunction with masonry as late as the 16th century.

It was in the 11th century that a true military architecture, with castles built entirely of masonry, first came into being; alongside these there existed many motte and bailey castles that had been more or less modified to meet the demands of the time. The nobles, who were extremely belligerent, were more concerned to protect themselves against surprise attacks than against set-piece sieges, which in any case had become extremely rare.

The small, irregular masonry used in the early fortresses gave way to the larger, more even masonry of the end of the 12th century, which had fine, neatly squared stones. Even an inexperienced eye can distinguish the two styles without any difficulty.

The keep became the most strictly military part of the fortress, while at the same time providing living quarters for the lord and his knights. The courtyard, which was the hub of life on the estate and a refuge for the population in time of war,

became customary to build narrow cruciform loop-holes high up in towers and curtains where walls were at their least thick; in addition the crossbow, which could be fired in a more confined space, took the place of the bow, before it was in turn superseded by firearms. 10. Loop-holes converted to take firearms. 11. Sectional view of a recessed loop-hole with (a) architectural features designed to deflect assailants' arrows. These defences are sometimes found in the shape of 'steps'. The height of the arrow-slit is not at all unusual – there are still some to be seen that are nearly 7 metres high. 12. Another type of loop-hole, this time without a recess, for use in small-scale defensive works.

HOARDING

1. Erecting a temporary hoard (early 12th century). 2. Permanent hoard made of masonry (13th century). The masonry was sometimes covered with slates for added protection. 3. Temporary hoarding below the roof of a 13th-century tower. A lighter version of the hoard shown in fig. 1 was built along ramparts, using the same straightforward construction method. 4. Double hoard, or a hoard built on two levels, which could be dismantled (early 13th century). 4a. View of inside of hoard. 4b. View of outside of hoard. 5. Temporary hoard supported by stone brackets from the keep at the castle of Coucy (13th century): a) loop-hole; b) machicolation; c) bowman in position at a loop-hole in a hoard. The hoards shown in all these figures had holes in the flooring through which stones, boiling liquid, etc., were thrown down on the enemy. This was, in fact, the most basic form of machicolation.

---

[1] The rogue became a hermit and died while on a pilgrimage of repentance to the Holy Land.
[2] At Andelys, in 1197.
[3] At Mont-Saint-Michel, in 1204.

1

2

3

4

a

b

a

b

6

c

5

a

b

c

L. & F. FUNCKEN

was surrounded by curtain walls that were often immensely thick and had, like the towers, a swelling base enabling them to deflect missiles and withstand undermining more readily. The rudiments of the defensive methods that were to be adapted and perfected from the 12th to the 15th century can be seen at Carcassonne – a virtual prototype of every major development that was to take place in this field.

We have already mentioned the castle of Pierrefonds; Haut-Koenigsburg, which has also come in for savage criticism, will give a reader travelling round the Vosges in Alsace a vivid impression of what a great German castle of the 15th century looked like. Although there is no comparison between such castles and the 'burgs' of the Rhine valley, the latter have become equally famous.

In Italy the Renaissance has left little of the Middle Ages surviving, but in Spain many interesting remains of the castles of the 'Reconquista' can still be seen in the imposing solitude of the Castilian plateau.

In England the 'White Tower' of London and its mysterious staircases take us back to the barbarous days of the Conquest. There is no other architectural evidence that goes back further than the end of the 14th century, except perhaps for the humble manor-houses[1] and the tiny peels, or fortified farms, found near the Scottish Borders. The tower and surrounding wall of these buildings, which provided a place of refuge for local farmers against raiders more intent on plunder than on murder, make them a pale reflection of the keeps of the beginning of the Middle Ages.

Poliorcetics

Poliorcetics, the learned term for the art of siege warfare, is derived from the Greek *poliorketikos* (from *poliorkein*, meaning to besiege a town). In Western Europe this art, which had begun to go into decline from the time of Clovis, had virtually died out by the end of the Viking invasions. That it reappeared

[1] The manor could not have towers or curtain walls. A large number of them existed in France, but they were unable to stand up to the ravages of the wars of the 15th and 16th centuries. Those that did survive were mostly razed to the ground during the 18th century.

SIEGE ENGINES (i)

1. Great trebuchet, also called the great trebuc; this drawing is based on the illustration by Viollet-le-Duc and the diagram by the 13th-century Picardian architect Villard de Honnecourt. The chronicler and poet Guillaume le Breton, writing during the same period, described the trebuchet as a kind of enormous sling. The counterweight (a), which was known as the bin, could hold 26 tonnes of earth. The shock absorbers (b) reduced the impact of the recoil when the engine was fired. The sling itself is shown at (c). Its adjusting rope (d), which was suspended from the eyelets (e) of the sling, produced the jolt that launched the projectile into the air; the nearer the rope was attached by the eyelets to the end of the beam, the more horizontal the angle of fire of the projectile became. The windlass (i) was used to pull down the beam, but a second windlass (j) first of all tightened the springs at (k) to the position shown by the grey outline. The second windlass (j), which had been wound up in the contrary direction, was then released and the springs, now that they had no pressure pulling them in, leapt apart, at the same time bringing the beam down from its vertical position. This initial lowering of the beam greatly facilitated the rest of the operation, which was completed by the first windlass (i). The beam, with its projectile on the end, was released by knocking out a pin (h) with a mallet (see figs. 2 and 3). Also to be noted are the groove for the sling (f); the pulley and release mechanism (g); the pin of the release mechanism (h); the ball, sometimes called the 'paunch' (l). 2. Detailed view of the release mechanism in open and closed position with its pulley (g) and pin (h). 3. The engine under tension (A); ready for firing (B); in stationary position after being fired (C) (g, h: see figs. 1 and 2). 4. Giant pivoting crossbow mounted on its three-wheeled carriage; a) sight mounted on an oval bearing, which provided a fixed point and a pivot for horizontal aiming. b) Olive-shaped roller which acted as a swivel for the carriage when the wheel (c) was raised out of the way in order to heighten the angle of fire. d) Stabilizers which meant that equal tension could be applied to both halves of the steel bow. Crossbows of smaller 'calibre' were also made, but these were strung by means of a windlass. The great crossbow, which was a manoeuvrable engine,

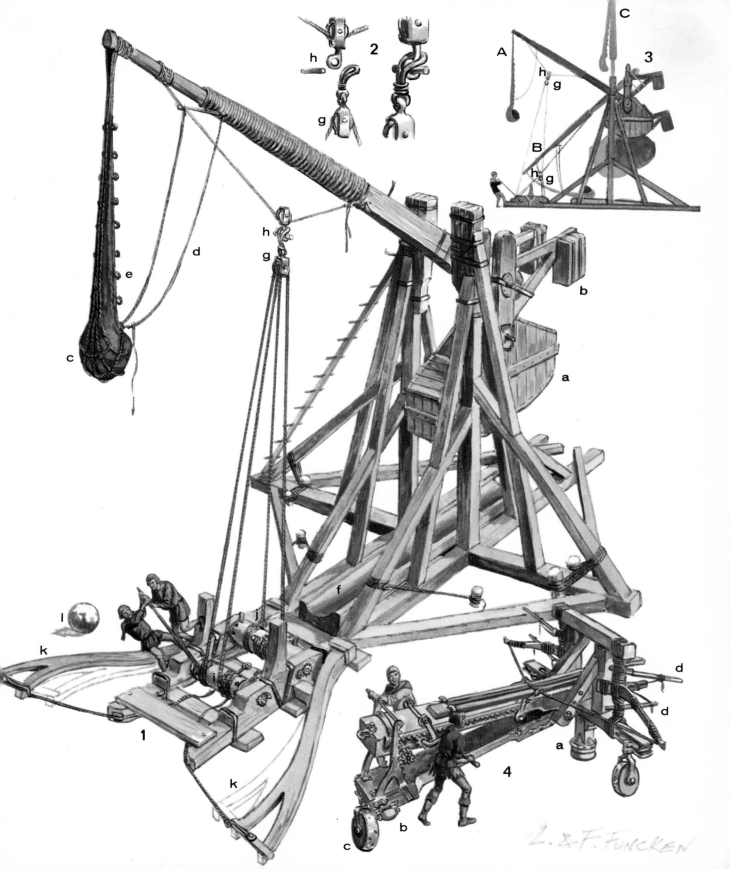

1

2

3

A

B

C

4

a

b

c

d

d

k

k

l

i

j

f

h

g

a

b

c

d

e

h

g

h

g

h

g

L. & F. Funcken

and flourished once more, in France as in the rest of Western Europe, was a direct result of the experience gained by the Crusaders while fighting against the siegecraft of the Byzantines, the Armenians and the Saracens. Engineers from Lombardy and Genoa had also preserved and even perfected the traditional techniques of the Roman armies; they played a large part in the capture of Nicea, Antioch and Jerusalem between the years 1097 and 1099.

Long sieges now became the rule whereas previously, under the primitive feudal system whereby levies could only be raised for a period of forty days on average a year, a noble could confidently feel himself to be invulnerable behind the impregnable walls of his fortress.

The king himself found it difficult to subdue the castles of his unruly vassals because of the lack of a standing army. From the 12th to the 15th centuries, from the reign of Philip Augustus to the time of Louis XI, the centralizing tendency of the French monarchy meant that ceaseless attempts were made to bring the feudal system under its control. However, at the same time as the art of siege warfare was developing, techniques of defence were also becoming more sophisticated, and in France, for example, these attained an astonishing degree of perfection. It could be said that defensive strategy remained superior to attacking strategy right up until the middle of the 15th century, and it was only improvements in artillery that destroyed the last remaining illusions of the barons and forced them to submit to the king's authority. [1]

Sapping and mining

The illustrations show the techniques involved in sapping and mining far better than any text can. From the 11th or 12th century onwards the most powerful Norman lords, like William the Conqueror's uncle at Arques, had galleries dug beneath the foundations of their fortresses on a level with the bottom of the moat so that the slightest noise of mine-working could be detected in time.

The troops of Philip Augustus already numbered among their ranks a corps of military engineers who directed teams of sappers, miners and navvies. These teams, which were re-

[1] Artillery also enabled Charles VII to recapture sixty fortifications from the English with far more ease than they had been taken shortly before.

was greatly feared on account of the power of its projectile, a boar-spear 5 metres long known as a 'garrot'. This could be fired directly up to a range of 50 metres. The pivoting crossbow was effective both against manned groups of infantry and cavalry, and against seige engines.

SIEGE ENGINES (ii)
1. The mangonel in a stationary position: a) wheels of the windlass; b) return pulleys; c) auxiliary windlass. This windlass (c) was used to hoist the firing rope (d) and its release mechanism (e) to the top end of the beam; the operation would have been too risky and too strenuous to be carried out by a member of the crew, and would also have exposed him to enemy fire. 2. Mangonel ready for firing. To activate it the 6-man crew worked the wheels (a) of the windlass and brought down the beam (g) by means of the return pulleys (b) and the firing rope (d). Next the pouch of the sling (f) and its projectile were hung from the end of the beam. The release mechanism (e) was then activated and the beam shot up, impelled by its counterweight (i). This movement was accentuated to a greater or lesser degree by the action of the men pulling down on the counterweight (here there are sixteen of them); they were given instructions by the 'chief engineer' who can be seen on the left of the picture. Besides stone balls, pebbles and incendiary material were also hurled at the enemy (h); even quantities of decaying carcasses were wrapped in nets and used as projectiles. Guillaume le Breton likened the mangonel to the Turkish perrier, a smaller and less powerful engine. 3. Catapult, known also as a scorpion. Although this was not so powerful as the more elaborate engines it had the advantage that it could be assembled from scratch on the spot, apart from the gearing and cranking-handles. If the metal parts were not available, the spring (made of green wood) could be wound up by using a winch linked to a simple system of pulleys. The frame pivoted on small wheels (a), so that horizontal aiming was possible. 3b. Detailed view of the system for vertical sighting.
4. Small trebuchet. The 'bible' was a light, simplified version of this engine that launched projectiles roughly the size of a man's fist. Its name is derived from *biblia*, the latin for a dice-box.

1

e
d
a
c
b

2

g
e
b
d
d
b
a
b

h

3b

3

a

a
c
i
a
f

4

cruited from among the mass of the populace who up until then had been barred from taking up arms, were raised only as they were needed.

The overhanging galleries and machicolations, of which we have shown several illustrations, were devised as a defence against sapping, and the sappers in turn protected themselves with a kind of portable roof which was called by a variety of names, e.g., 'sow', 'cat', 'vine', etc.

Sapping was so effective, and so much feared (with good reason) that many a fortress surrendered before the saps had been set alight; this happened, for instance, at the castle of La Roche-Guyon which was besieged by the English in 1419. It was customary for the besieger to invite the besieged enemy to come and see with his own eyes whether the saps were indeed ready to be fired; often, once his 'evident ruin had been shown to him', the unfortunate castellan chose to surrender.

Mining, which took a great deal longer to carry out, had the enormous advantage of being concealed from the enemy throughout most of the operation, thereby achieving complete surprise.

In order to forestall this terrible threat, architects would sometimes have a countermine dug in advance; the miners from the besieging forces would emerge into these galleries – little suspecting the warm reception that lay in store for them. Where the gallery of the besiegers' mine passed under the gallery of a countermine, a vertical shaft would be dug and water poured down it so as to drown the miners. The famous keep at Coucy had a spring at ground level in the gallery of its countermine which provided an abundant supply of water for this very purpose.

When this valuable asset was lacking, all the besieged forces could do was dig a countermine and try to link up with the enemy gallery. This, in fact, is the course of action that was most usually adopted, and it resulted in countless bitter hand-to-hand battles fought out by the flickering light of a lantern. On occasions these surprise encounters took a chivalrous turn and many a great lord claimed the right to fight underground – against a worthy opponent, of course.

At the siege of Melun in 1420 a series of remarkable combats took place in just such a manner, at the junction of a mine and a countermine.[1] After the miners from both camps had built a

[1] *Chronicle of Charles VI*, by Jean II Juvenal des Ursins (1388–1473).

SIEGES (i)

1. Sapping. After advancing along an open trench (A, shown in section), then under cover of a kind of floor (B, seen from above), the sappers have loosened the stone of the outer facing of the wall (C) and are digging out the rubble from inside. This method of building walls with a rubble core, a legacy from the period of the late Roman Empire, lasted until the 12th century, when it began to be replaced by a more uniform and better finished method of construction that made the work of the sapper more difficult. Sometimes the base of the wall was widened to form an embankment; however the most ingenious method of all (which admittedly was only rarely encountered) consisted of constructing the upper part of the wall so that it rested on relieving arches (D), which in turn were supported by reinforced and well-protected foundations. Sapping was completely ineffective against these measures. Apart from this procedure the only way to counteract sapping was to erect a second wall (E) behind the section that was threatened, or, if there were no stones available, to build a wooden breteche (see the double-page spread on siege engines). 2. Once the sap had been completed and shored up with props, faggots covered with an inflammable substance (sometimes just lard was used) were piled up in the gap. The fire burned away the props and the wall collapsed. This was known as mining with firebrands, and was not to be replaced by mining with gunpowder until the beginning of the 16th century. 3. Battering-ram. In the illustration we have stripped away most of its protective covering so that the basic structure can be seen. It was operated by eight, ten or twelve men, depending on the size of the ram, who swung the ram backwards and forwards so as to set up a pendulum-like movement that had formidable destructive power. 4. Basic rock drill, and a fast-action rock drill driven by a bow. The operators of these engines were protected overhead by 'cats', 'sows' and other types of covered gallery.

B

E

C

D   D

A

1

2

3

4

L. & F.
FUNCKEN

solid barrier, they withdrew to make way for a whole procession of noble warriors who came to challenge the enemy and fight with cold steel. King Henry V of England and many noble lords were spectators at this crude joust; they dispensed words of praise and even knighted several of the fighters.

This bizarre episode, which seems more reminiscent of a novel than of war, shows the extent to which the old spirit of chivalry had declined. Armand Guilhem de Barbazan, the commander of the castle, who was later to be dubbed 'the perfect knight' by Charles VII but who today is quite forgotten, was imprisoned for eight years after the surrender of the castle in company with a good many others,[1] while several of his comrades-in-arms 'who had friends and acquaintances among the Burgundians' returned home as free men.

In his *Quadrilogue Invectif* Alain Chartier[2] deplored the attitude of those lords who were only interested in jousting and shameful wheeling and dealing, accusing them of ruining the country instead of defending it, of hiring themselves out to the highest bidder, be he French or Burgundian, and always being ready to betray their latest master.

This insouciant nobility who chafed against the discipline and discomfort of camp life often refused to serve under an experienced captain. Protected by heavy suits of armour (and we should remember that armour was reaching a state of near-perfection at the time), these arrogant lords had all the confidence of veterans. Chartier said of them; 'Each one wants to be a company and a leader on his own. And there are so many captains and masters-at-arms that they can hardly all find squires and varlets.[3] Nowadays, knowing how to buckle on a sword or put on armour is enough to make a man a captain'.

In this particularly turbulent period of French history, Joan of Arc managed for a brief moment to embody the aspirations of a people who were exhausted both by the civil wars forced on them by the overweening nobility and by the destruction that the English conquest had brought in its wake. Yet Joan became the point around which the idea of patriotism and nationhood crystallized.

[1] He was later released by La Hire, died in battle at Bulgnéville in 1432 and was buried in Saint-Denis with full military pomp.

[2] Chartier, who was born in 1385 and died in 1433, was secretary to Charles VI and Charles VII.

[3] Chartier is referring here to the impossibility of forming a 'lance', which was a basic strategic unit. See Part I, pp. 54 ff.

SIEGES (ii): MINING

1. Diagram of a mine: a) wall; c) gallery; d) chamber of the mine; e) props. 2. Sectional view of a mine: a) wall; b) moat; c) sloping gallery in case the enemy counter-attack by flooding the mine; d) chamber of the mine; e) props arranged in a gallows-frame; f) fence erected as a means of defence and also as a camouflage to hide the works in progress. Ideally, houses situated near the target were used as shelter during operations. Once the works were completed, the procedure was the same as for sapping. As soon as the props had been burned away, the masonry weighing down on the outer facing of the wall, which had been further weakened by the underground work, suddenly collapsed. The debris fell into the moat, forming a bank by which the assault column could enter the fortress. The technique of undermining was far more complex than that used in sapping (see previous plate) and required the cooperation of a highly skilled team of assistants; it did, however, have the advantage that the besieged enemy knew nothing of the operation while it was being carried out. The men of the provinces of Northern France and Brabant were especially skilled in the art of mining. Quite a large number of fortifications dating from the 12th to the 14th centuries still bear the scars of this method of attack, in particular the walled town of Carcassonne, in southern France, where several partially blocked-up mine galleries were found.

3. Sectional view of a mine gallery designed for direct assault which enabled troops to burst into the fortress under cover of dark: a) wall; b) moat; c) gallery; d) the depth of the shored-up soil remaining prior to the moment of attack. Ideally this type of mine would be built in the vicinity of a gate. The assault group would put the guards on the gate out of action, raise the portcullis, and lower the drawbridge so that the main attack column could storm the stronghold.

4. The only way to detect mining operations was to stand watch over bowls filled with water; any activities by miners down below would cause ripples to form on the surface, and a counter-mine could immediately be dug.

5. *Chapels de fer*, known as kettle-hats. Sappers, miners and navvies all wore this highly popular type of military headgear; their version however, had a specially wide brim.

SIEGES (iii)

1. Bastille made of clay and wattle frames. At its foot can be seen the opening to the tunnel through which the telescopic cat protecting the sappers has been moved; the moat has already been filled in.

2. Sapper's cat, also called a 'vine', with winches to move it forward. These wooden engines were usually protected against the risk of fire by a covering of newly-flayed hides; turf, or even dung, were also used on occasion, but metal plates were a rare luxury. The men working the winches were evidently shielded from the fire of the besieged enemy by wooden or wicker screens.

3. Gallery of an ordinary sap.

4. Wicker siege-basket.

5. Mantlets. Archers and crossbowmen played a crucial role in sieges. The hail of arrows they put up was directed at stopping the defenders from taking up a position in threatened parts of the fortress. These front-line sharpshooters were the prime target of the besieged troops and so had to use a whole range of easily transportable screens for protection.

6. *Charcloie* or mobile mantlet.

7. Attacking by means of scaling the fortress wall with ladders (known as an 'escalade'). This speedy method of attack was used by a few of the great commanders, among them du Guesclin, and called for brave and determined men. However it raised an almost universal outcry, even among the companions of the famous du Guesclin, who was accused of 'spoiling the art of war'.

8. A 'castle-cat', or '*chat-chastel*', has just failed in its attempt to force the drawbridge of the barbican. The men whose job was to manoeuvre the battering ram are trying to break free from their post, the 'cat' section of the 'castle'.

9. Rampart 'crow'. A similar type of huge hook, this time suspended from ropes, was used to grab hold of the head of battering rams housed in engines known as 'sheep'. Appropriately enough this hook was called a 'wolf'.

10. Engine known as a 'cat' or 'stork', which was sometimes mounted on wheels. It could of course only be used when the enemy was caught unawares and unprepared.

11. Ladder with movable struts. It was housed in high wattle mantlets to protect it as it was moved forward. Sliding ladders with extending sections like the ones used by firemen today were also used.

12. Sapper's 'mouse' (from the Latin *musculus*). This was used in the same way as a mantlet to enable troops to get near a wall that was to be sapped; it was then turned round so that the sappers could work in the safety of its cover.

13. Breteche hastily erected to repair the damage to part of a curtain wall that has collapsed as a result of sapping operations. The assault troops have been brought to an abrupt halt by this unexpected obstacle. Originally the term 'breteche' was applied to the defences and towers of palisaded enclosures; later it was used to mean the overhanging galleries of wood or stone that guarded gates or other openings (see the plate depicting the castle).

14. Small *chat-chastel* or 'falcon', known also as a 'crane'.

15. Assault tower called a *beffroy* or *chat-chastiau* when it had a compartment for transporting sappers in its base, and a 'sow' when it was fitted with devices for throwing missiles. These enormous engines were propelled by the same methods as those in fig. 2.

16. Small artillery pieces for use on ramparts. One of them has just hurled a barrel of incendiary material at the assault tower. In addition to this vast panorama of human ingenuity we should mention some rare specimens of frogmen's diving suits, which were black and had a primitive breathing-mask attached. The engines depicted here were used extensively by every fighting nation. The German Zeitblom, who lived in the 15th century, has left behind valuable drawings of some of these machines, as have the anonymous illustrators of, for example, *La Pyrotechnie de l'Ancelot Lorrain*, the *Walturius*, the *Recueil d'anciens poètes*, and the *Noticia Utraque cum Orientis tum Occidentis*. Other writers of the 15th and 16th centuries also left behind a large number of drawings of these machines, done in vertical section and based on very old diagrams; however they are so wildly imaginative and so obviously lacking in technical knowledge that only a few fragmentary indications of what the original diagrams contained (these, unfortunately, are probably lost for good) can be found in them. Many early drawings of siege machines are merely the product of an overfertile imagination, like, for example, the enormous bladed wheel armed with crossbows drawn by that whimsical genius, the great Leonardo da Vinci.

BALLISTIC ENGINES

1. Light catapult with springs made of steel blades, from a 15th century drawing by Zeitblom.

1a. The catapult when released.

2. Small trebuchet (early 15th century). Note the four possible positions for the peg securing the release mechanism; this meant that the range of the engine could be regulated with a fair degree of accuracy.

3. *Ribauldequin* dating from the mid-14th century. Some armies used as many as several hundred of these weapons at a time. Juvénal des Ursins estimated that the Duke of Burgundy's army had 2,000 of them in use in 1411. This drawing is done to the same scale as fig. 2.

4. Ballista or perrier, known also as a *chaable*. The Turkish perrier was a similar type of engine, though lighter and less powerful. The perdreaus used by the French against the Flemish at the battle of Mons-en-Pévèle in 1304 were probably small-calibre perriers using fist-sized stone balls as ammunition. Early writers tended to mistake the great trebuchet for the ballista.

fortification led engineers to devise machines more powerful than the ballista. The result of this was the invention of the trebuchet, a type of engine that worked on the principle of the counterbalanced spring. From the time of the first Crusade, 'engingneurs' like the Genoese Guglielmo and Primo Embriarco, or the Armenian Havedic, were renowned for their skill at building and manipulating these huge machines. The valuable services of specialists like these could only be secured by paying a high price and by satisfying additional demands that were often nothing more than whims.

The type of projectile that was used varied enormously. As well as blocks of rough or hewn stone, incendiary devices were also used, for example 'pochonnets' (small containers made of glass or earthenware), 'grenades'[1] and 'poison bottles' that hurled powdered quicklime, explosive material, grape-shot, asphyxiating gases, and even the heads of decapitated prisoners (an early form of psychological warfare![2]) at the enemy.

Cannon

As early as the 13th century the forces of Gengis Khan were using weapons which were known in medieval Europe as vases, 'fire pots' or 'iron pots'. They did not appear in Europe until the beginning of the 14th century, and were first reported in Italy (in Tuscany, to be exact), and later in the south of Germany. These weapons were also encountered in Flanders, in 1314, and a few years later, between 1321 and 1326, in England and in France. It would be pointless, however, to try and establish any sort of order of precedence in what was probably one of the earliest occurrences of the 'arms race' in Europe. What is beyond question is that the western nations armed themselves with cannon more or less simultaneously.

The first French text to contain an undisputed reference to artillery proper dates from 1338. The passage in question concerns a bombard which is described as 'an iron pot for shooting fire-arrows, or "garrots", forty-eight garrots with

[1] The Saracens made extensive use of oil. Traces of mercury found in missiles suggest that they might have been acquainted with mercury fulminate, a powerful explosive that is still in use today.
[2] It was practised by the gallant crusaders in Palestine.

ARTILLERY (ii)

1. The Tannenberg gun, unearthed during the last century from the ruins of the castle of the same name that was besieged and destroyed in 1399 by the militias of Mainz and Frankfurt. This hand-gun, which was cast in bronze, is 32 cm long and has a calibre of 14.5 mm. It shows the degree of craftsmanship attained by some gunmakers who were well in advance of their time; the quality of their work anticipated the skills of gunmakers of a century later. Sectional view of the gun showing the touch-hole, the charge, the ball and the wad and tow.

2. Vertical touch-hole with its priming pan.

3. Second type of touch-hole, this time located at the side of the barrel, with its small priming pan.

4. Second type of serpentine (the first example is shown in the previous plate) which was adopted around the mid-15th century. It was also known as a 'dragon', or 'dog' – names which were later applied to flintlock weapons and which have continued in use right up until the present day.

5. Third type of serpentine, with a touch-hole cover to protect it from the wind and rain, second half of the 15th century.

6. Fourth type, of German make, with a spring-loaded trigger, a foresight, a firing pan and cover (made in 1475). This was a revolutionary weapon in its day.

7. Culverineer on horseback (c.1470). This extremely primitive weapon, known as a 'petronel', was used in conjunction with serpentine guns up until the beginning of the 16th century.

7a. Detailed drawing of the gun's mounting. The operator could remove the cotter pin for faster reloading.

8. In the mid-15th century the absence of the serpentine was compensated for by providing the incendarius (shooter) with an assistant, the collineator (gun-layer).

9. Hand-gun from the early 15th century. Some pieces that were too heavy or too powerful to be fired from the shoulder were operated in this manner. Similar types of gun have been found dating from the same period, but these are less well made and mounted on wood.

10. An Italian mercenary in the pay of the king of France (late 15th century). He is armed with a 'fire-lance'.

10a. The fire-lance seen in cross section. This device, which was bound together with iron wire, consisted of a hollow wooden cylinder containing a narrow iron tube. It was filled with several charges, each of which consisted of a portion of gunpowder

detachable steel and feather tips, a pound of saltpeter and half a pound of live sulphur to make powder to fire the afore-mentioned garrots'. Similarly, the 'thunder tubes for firing garrots' that were used by the town of Lille in 1340 unmistakably refer to cannons firing arrows. In fact the garrot was nothing more than an enormous incendiary arrow, and although this strange missile was quickly superseded by the stone cannonball, it remained in use until the end of the 16th century.

The rapid developments that took place in methods of casting cannon made it possible for a more suitable projectile to be used, namely the stone cannonball. This in turn was soon being challenged by the cast iron cannonball, despite the fact that it was far more costly and used up more powder. These twin disadvantages resulted in the stone cannonball remaining in use until the end of the 15th century. However the metal cannonball, whose unit mass was nearly three times as great, was to make possible a gradual reduction in the calibre of cannon; at the same time improvements in the manufacture of gunpowder enabled the kinetic force of the projectile to be maintained. This area, however, is to be discussed later.

Before these true cannon arrived on the scene, the arsenal in the first half of the 14th century contained only small-calibre guns that were quite incapable of rivalling the effectiveness of the great ballistic engines with their large teams of skilled operators.

Bombards

The first 'quennons'[1] were cast in iron, copper, bronze or brass, and were made in a single piece, by a similar process to that used in bellmaking. As techniques of casting were still too crude to produce heavy-calibre weapons, ingenious craftsmen introduced a new method of manufacture: they made 'heavy calibres' out of strips of wrought iron bound tightly together with hoops, after the fashion of barrels. The illustrations show in detail how this was done.

Thus the bombard was invented (according to its etymology the name means 'which makes a noise'). The shorter version, intended for indirect firing, was called a mortar

[1] The term was first encountered in 1348. The word cannon, which is supposed to be derived from the Latin *canna*, meaning reed, seems in our opinion more likely to come from the German *Kanne*, meaning pot or can.

on top of which was placed a ball of tow impregnated with gunpowder, followed by four fingers of gross powder mixed with Greek fire, ground glass, coarse salt, saltpetre, and iron filings; next came a new charge of gunpowder, a lead ball, and so on up to the muzzle of the barrel, where the whole thing was ignited. This Roman candle concoction was responsible for burning down houses and crops, terrifying horses and throwing groups of footsoldiers into total disarray.

ARTILLERY (iii)

1. Earliest known picture of a cannon, taken from the English manuscript of Walter de Millimete, dated 1326. There are some experts who have vigorously challenged this date; they deny that the touch-hole could have been in existence at this time and question the use here of the red-hot firing rod. Contrary to widespread opinion this rod appears to us to be a match-holder, as the enlarged drawing in fig. 1a (which is a faithful copy of the original) clearly demonstrates. On the other hand the knight's costume, which has sometimes been thought to date from the period after 1326, is in fact an old-fashioned style of dress that was being worn in Continental Europe fifty years earlier. It is also worth pointing out that the lions on the ailettes protecting the knight's shoulders are of an archaic design; moreover these defensive plates, though very common elsewhere, were very rarely depicted in English manuscripts. The unlikely shape of the gun-carriage is proof that the illustrator only had a brief, written description of the new weapon to work from. 1b. A 14th-century cannon, probably the oldest known specimen. This is the sort of weapon that the author of the illumination in fig. 1 was most probably attempting to portray.

1c. The crudely-drawn projectile in fig. 1 could never have been actually fired. A bas-relief in Edinburgh Castle dating from the 16th century was of great help to us in our attempts to draw one of these iron bolts with its leather wad. Incidentally they were still being used two centuries later as incendiary devices. 1d. Fire-arrow, approximately 1.5 metres long (second half of the 16th century). The detachable flighted section was probably intended to make it more difficult to remove the flaming arrow once it had reached its target. (Taken from the manuscript of *L'Art de l'artillerie* by Wolff de Senftenberg, chief of artillery at Danzig).

2. English mortar forged around 1346; it is 1.22 metres long and has a calibre of approximately 50 cm. 3. Wrought-iron bombard fitted with trunnions. The trunnions (a) made vertical sighting easier and absorbed the worst of the recoil; they are generally thought to have been invented around 1450–1470. We have taken the drawing of a bombard with its trunnions attached to one of its binding-hoops from an illumination in one of the manuscript versions of the *Livre de Marco Polo*, written around 1400 (the clothing worn by the characters corroborates this date). 4. *Veuglaire* with a movable firing chamber or box. 4a. Cross-section of the chamber loaded with gunpowder and sealed with a wooden tampion; also shown is the chase with its projectile and wad. 4b. The chamber of the cannon wedged into the breech. 5. Trunnioned *veuglaire* with movable box (a), support (b) and locking-pin (c). On the left of the picture is a detailed view of the chamber (a) above its support (b), with the locking-pin (c) of the breech. 6. Breech with cheeks (late 15th century); also shown are the locking-pins (a) and locking-wedge (b). 7. Breech fitted with a hinge locking-bar and locking wedge (a) (late 15th century). 8. Breech-bolt fitted with a stirrup handle (late 15th century). 9. Breech-loading 'organ'-type ribaudequin with six barrels cast in iron; in Germany this was known as a *Todtenorgel* (organ of death). During the previous century this engine was fitted with pikes instead of gun-barrels; the 'organ' model was used to defend the corners of fortified camps. 9a. Detail showing an open breech next to a breech that has been closed with a square breech-plug and pin; this method was frequently used in multi-barrelled artillery pieces. 10. Muzzle-loading five-barrelled ribaudequin of German make (c.1450).

ARTILLERY (iv)

1. Early 15th-century bombard set in its trough-shaped bed.
2. Great bombard mounted on its chest-type gun-carriage (15th century). This type of mounting was used in siege warfare until the opening decades of the 16th century. The guns in figs. 1 and 2 both have a touch-hole fuse for holding the priming powder. This method prevented the mouth of the touch-hole from becoming damaged, or at least retarded the process considerably.
3. During sieges artillerymen were shielded from enemy fire either by mantlets fixed in position or, as shown here, by a swinging door with an embrasure for the gun. The stoutly-built contraption for absorbing the shock of the gun's recoil can also be seen in the illustration. No wall could withstand for long the heavy projectiles of these great bombards, which many people today still refuse to take seriously. Yet the mere sight of them was often enough to make entire garrisons surrender – and those men knew what they were up against. To give an example, the fortress of Tannenberg (which was mentioned on one of the previous plates) saw one of its curtain walls crumble away at the second bombardment by one of the Frankfurt cannons. To the left of the gun can be seen a powder ladle and a rammer of the period.
4. Gun-carriage in two sections articulated below the muzzle (c.1450). During aiming the whole weight of the gun was supported by the upper part of the structure.
5. Cannon mounted on a gun-carriage built in one piece, with the movable firing chamber wedged in position. Beside it is a chamber ready for use. 6. Gun-carriage in two sections, articulated behind the breech (c.1470). This made aiming much less difficult, as most of the weight of the gun rested on the axle. 7. Chest containing powder cartridges. A reference to this invention, which is usually thought to be of a much more recent date, has been found in a manuscript dating from the second half of the 15th century.

8. Mortar. The illuminators of the 15th century have left us very few accurate drawings of gun-carriages. Mortars in particular are always shown suspended in this improbable and incomplete fashion – incomplete because the effect of the recoil would inevitably have been to wrench the gun from its precarious perch. It is interesting to note in passing that the industrious illustrators of the period were seemingly quite unaware of how invaluable their evidence would have been to researchers in later centuries, and were never tempted to paint these massive guns. In actual fact mortars had to be embedded in an almost vertical position in a kind of huge trough and aimed with the help of wedges in order to obtain the required angle of elevation.
9. Ribauldequin from the mid-15th century. This weapon can be considered the ancestor of the modern self-propelled gun, the characteristic features of which it already has, namely a barrel, armour-plating and propulsion. The name of this engine is sometimes attributed to the 'ribalds', or servants whose job it was to man the giant crossbow with which the machine was originally armed. The accounts of the town of Bruges for the year 1340 describe this weapon as a 'new engine'.

ARTILLERY (v)

1. Method of laying a cannon (late 15th century). 2. 'Mons Meg' mounted on its gun-carriage. The largest of the bombards, which were designed to smash holes in fortress walls, were fixed to a stout wooden framework or gun-carriage; because of their enormous weight there was no possibility of vertical aiming. Nevertheless we should mention here a bas-relief in Edinburgh Castle which shows an artilleryman's quadrant in the muzzle of 'Mons Meg', with a wooden wedge used for aiming by the breech; one wonders, however, what was used to raise such a huge mass. 'Mons Meg' was fired for the last time in 1682 (a blank, of course) in honour of the arrival in Scotland of the Duke of York, the future king James II of England. The cannon was loaded with an excessive amount of gunpowder of a far more powerful type than that used in the mid-15th century, with the result that two of its binding hoops snapped and it was damaged at the rear of the bore, just at the point where the screw of the chamber begins (see fig. D). Mons Meg was then left abandoned and neglected until 1754, when it was consigned to the Tower of London with some other old cannons that were no longer in use. In 1829, as a direct result of the patriotic efforts of Sir Walter Scott, the bombard was brought back to Edinburgh, where it continues to astound the tourists.

Giant bombards: A. Bombard from Burgundy, emblazoned with the coat of arms of Auxy and erroneously said to belong to Louis XI; captured by the Swiss after the battle of Morat in 1476. Length: 2.75 m. Weight: 2,000 kilos. Calibre: 36.5 cm. Weight of projectile: 50 kilos. B. English cannon captured by the French at Mont-Saint-Michel, and called a 'Michelette' in French. Length: 3.53 m. Weight: 3,500 kilos. Calibre: 37 cm. Weight of cannonball: 75 kg. C. English 'Michelette'. Length: 3.64 m. Weight: 5,500 kilos. Calibre: 45 cm. Weight of projectile: 150 kilos. These are without doubt the earliest bombards that have survived to this day. They were probably built in Flanders, though exactly when we cannot say, and abandoned by the English after they failed to destroy the fortifications of Mont-Saint-Michel in 1434. D. 'Mons Meg', forged in Belgium by J. Cambier in 1449 and sent to James II of Scotland by Philip the Good of France in 1457. Length: 3.90 m. Weight: 6,600 kilos. Calibre: 50 cm. Weight of projectile: 150 kilos. In his book entitled *Guns*, Erich Egg claims that the stone balls had a range of approximately 263 metres. Another type of projectile, made of metal this time, had a range of only 129 metres because of its greater weight – if we are to believe a contemporary manuscript. E. 'Dulle Griet' ('Mad Margaret'), a bombard made in Ghent, dating from the mid-15th century. It was captured in 1452 at the siege of Oudenarde by a Burgundian relieving army, and was retaken by main force by Ghentish troops in 1578. Length: 5.025 m. Weight: 16,400 kilos. Calibre: 64 cm. Weight of projectile: 340 kilos. F. 'Great Gun of Mahomet II' or the 'Dardanelles Cannon', cast in bronze for the Turks, probably in 1464. It was presented to Britain by Sultan Abdül-Aziz in 1867. Length: 5.25 m. Weight: 7,500 kilos. Calibre: 66 cm. Weight of projectile: 360 kilos. Cannons D, E and F could be unscrewed at the point where the firing chamber joined the chase by means of levers inserted into the slots visible on most of the models shown here. In the opinion of Ffoulkes, the English expert on cannon, figs. B and C belong to the same family of guns, although the cannons themselves are too badly damaged for there to be any concrete evidence of this. Fig. A has slots which would seem to indicate the presence of a screw thread; however, the cannon has not been examined closely enough for this to be stated with any degree of certainty. It is unlikely that this could have been used simply for greater ease of loading. It was more probably intended to make the transport of these immensely heavy guns easier by dividing them into two sections. All the cannons shown here can still be seen today and they bear witness to the extraordinary virtuosity of the craftsmen of the period, in this as in so many other areas. Their achievements are astounding and suggest that we might be a little more modest about our own modern products, which are manufactured with the aid of technical resources that are effective and sophisticated in a different kind of way. G. A bombard-cum-mortar known as the 'Turin bombard', made of cast iron (c.1420). Length: 1.44 m. Weight: 1,500 kilos. Calibre: 51 cm. Weight of projectile: 100 kilos. H. The 'Steyr bombard' (Austrian), dating from the first half of the 15th century. Length: 2.58 m. Weight: 7,100 kilos. Calibre: 80 cm. Weight of projectile: 700 kilos. I. Method of manufacturing cannons in wrought iron (figs. A, B, C, E and H). Iron rods are placed longitudinally next to one another around a wooden mandril – like the staves of a barrel – and then tightly bound together by a series of iron hoops applied at white heat. Figs. A to H are drawn to the same scale: the human figure at the bottom of the page gives some idea of their size in relation to a man 1.70 metres tall. The red line indicates the shape of the chase with the firing chamber and touch-hole at the rear end.

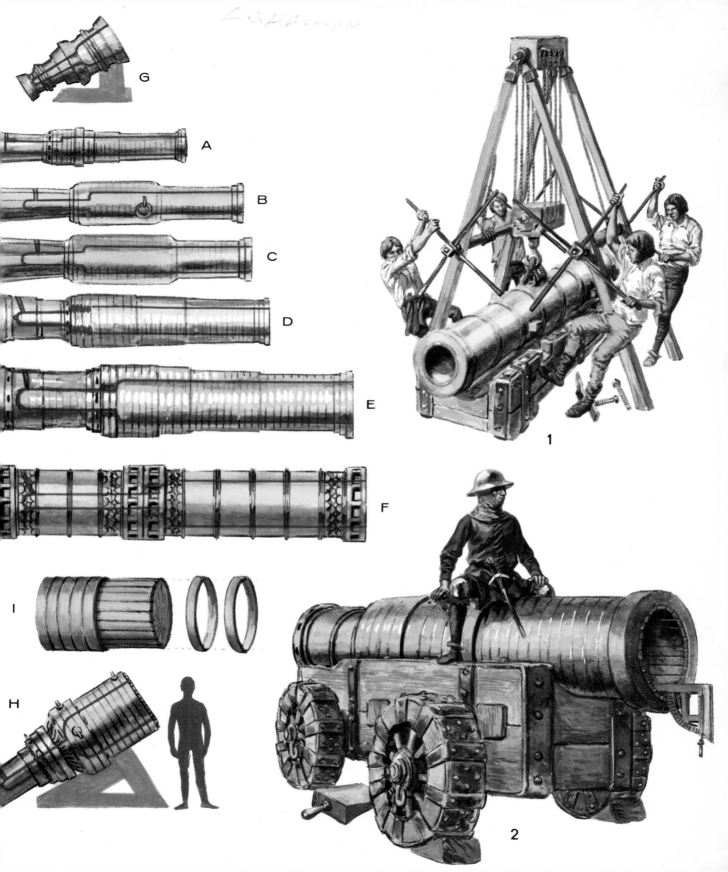

G

A

B

C

D

E

F

I

H

1

2

because it resembled the alchemist's mortar in shape. The small bombard, with its cone-shaped barrel, was termed a 'bombardelle'. The patience, common sense and tremendous technical skill which the craftsmen of the period showed in devising these weapons still command the admiration of metallurgists today.

The 'veuglaire'

Taken from the Latin *fulgurare*, meaning to strike with a thunderbolt, the word 'veuglaire'[1] was the term for a type of medium-calibre cannon; it was extremely easy to handle, and had the distinctive feature of a detachable box or chamber for holding gunpowder. The veuglaire was first built in the same way as the bombard, but later was cast in iron and, from 1450 onwards, in bronze. This type of cannon, which probably came into existence around 1400, continued to be used until the mid-16th century; however, models still in use at that time often dated from the previous century.

We would be wrong to underestimate the effectiveness of these weapons. It was one of these cannon that in 1435 took off the top of the skull of Jacques de Lalaing, known as the 'Good Knight', with a carefully-aimed shot. This man, who was one of the most famous 'professional tourneyers' in Europe, had lost his way during the siege of the castle of Poucques.

Hand guns

Although the idea of using miniature cannon seems perfectly natural to us, it was not put into practice until relatively late on, due to prejudice, habit and, above all, the aversion felt by knights towards a weapon which overturned all the rules and values of medieval warfare.

As a result the use of 'gunpowder shafts', Italian 'scopetes' or 'hand guns' – the *Fustbusse* (*Faustbüchsen*) of the Germans – first developed among the lower ranks of troops. They are found, under a variety of names, first of all in Italy, then in Germany, Flanders and Brussels, from where mercenaries hired by the king of England set out in 1314.

The new weapon had an enormous advantage over the bow and the crossbow in that it did not require any special care or

---

[1] Some authors prefer to regard the word as a corruption of the Flemish *vogeleer* or the German *Vogler*, meaning fowler. The spelling 'veughelaire' can be found in a French text dated 1412.

40

maintenance; in addition it could be made in half a day and was much cheaper.[1] The lead bullets were easy to cast and could be produced at the rate of twelve a minute. The weapon had only one drawback: its range was barely 50 metres at the beginning of the 15th century – yet it could pierce a suit of armour at 20 metres.

Eye-witnesses of the time were impressed by the effectiveness of a salvo fired by a disciplined unit. Thus in 1430 Pietroni Belli described the devastating effect of bullets, which were capable of passing right through two to three unarmoured men. Crack shots were not unknown at the time either. One of them, a Lorrainer called Maître Jean, killed a large number of English soldiers during the siege of Rouen in 1428.

As far back as 1450, French culverins were mowing down the formidable English archers. Gunpowder promised to be the invention that was going to decisively and irresistibly change, and eventually revolutionize, traditional methods of combat. We will continue our study of its development in Part III.

---

[1] An English document of 1353 gives a price of 3 shillings for a small-bore barrel and reckons the cost of a large crossbow to be 66 shillings.

II ARMOUR

Hauberks and habergeons

In Part I we described the equipment worn by the knights of early medieval times and traced the development of the byrnie to its final form of a garment of mail covering the entire body.

The hauberk

'Hauberk' is the term universally applied today to the garment in the shape of a hooded tunic which was worn for several centuries until eventually it came to be reinforced with pieces of leather or metal; these gradually increased in number and were designed to be more and more close-fitting.

We cannot allow to go unmentioned here François Buttin's views on the subject,[1] which are aimed at restoring the true meaning of the word 'hauberk'. The hauberk, which is derived from the German *Hals*, meaning a throat, and *bergen*, meaning to hide or protect, was the piece of equipment, typically shaped like a hood, covering the head and the upper part of the torso. The privilege of wearing it was restricted to knights only.

One of the many proofs of this is provided for us by the famous chronicler, Jean, Lord of Joinville (1224–1317), who lived during the reign of Saint Louis of France. In his *Mémoires* he gives as an explanation for his absence at the battle of Taillebourg in 1242, the fact that he was not entitled to wear the hauberk, as he was only nominated a knight in 1245: 'For I had on that occasion no hauberk'.

During those troubled and violent times the social framework in time of peace was the same as in time of war. The great feudal lords were attended by their barons, who were

[1] *Military Costume of the Middle Ages and the Renaissance*

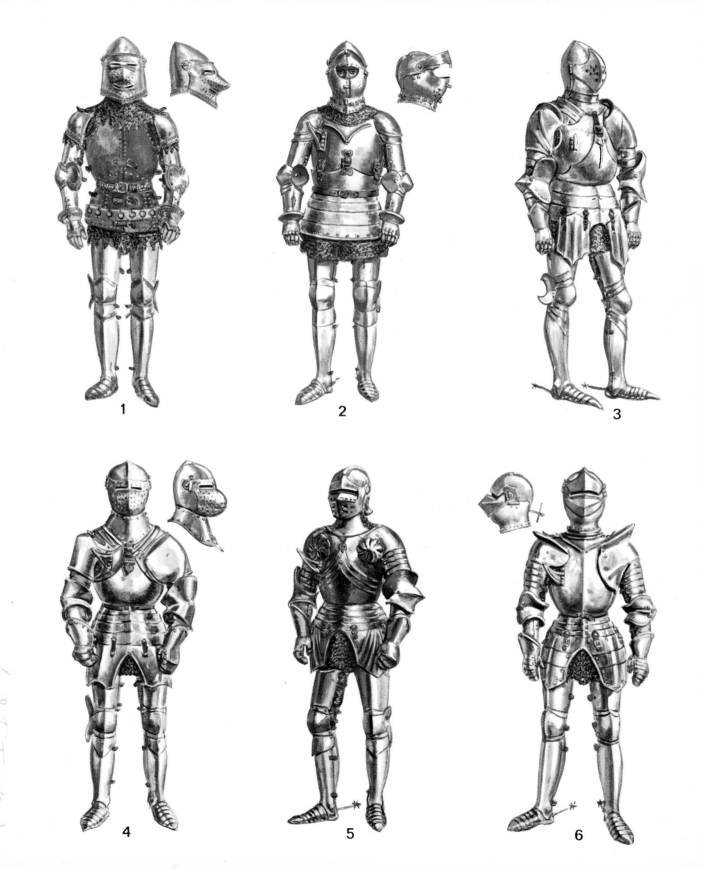

1   2   3

4   5   6

themselves accompanied by their knights banneret, who in turn gathered together knights bachelor under their banner. The latter, who made up the core of the lance (the tactical and organizational unit of the army[1]), each held a fief known as a 'knight's fief' or, more interestingly, a 'hauberk fief' on which he lived. If the hauberk had in fact been the famous 'coat of mail', this term would have been entirely meaningless, since all ranks of the army were entitled to wear one.

The hauberk, which was worn with the conical helmet, disappeared from use with the adoption of the bascinet. This type of helmet, which fitted the head more closely and was normally worn with an aventail minus its coif, could be recognized by the staples which held it in position. From this time on, the hauberk gradually lost its symbolic significance, and became 'public property' in the 14th century, when it was worn by the humblest sections of the army.

The habergeon

Although nowadays the habergeon (from the Old French *haubert-gone*[2]) is thought of as a kind of small hauberk, it was in fact a garment reaching to the knees that had fitted sleeves and a hood covering the head. It was the first wartime uniform, and from the time of the 12th century the wearing of it was compulsory and enforced by charter; it only disappeared from use in the second half of the 16th century. This is the garment to which the term 'hauberk' has been applied in recent times, and it has formed the subject of a lengthy and scholarly discussion by François Buttin.

By way of a more modest contribution to this argument, we quote here an illustrated passage taken from the *Pilgrimage of Human Life* [*Pèlerinage de la vie humaine*] (a work dating from the end of the 13th century), which supports Buttin's thesis. The extract gives an account of a man-at-arms preparing for battle and donning the various parts of his equipment one by one. The habergeon is depicted in the illustrations (along with the phrase 'Thus I don the habergeon') as a long, heavy tunic, identical in every respect to our modern 'hauberk', and not at all a 'hauberk of small size'.

This would make an interesting topic of discussion for philologists!

[1] This definition of the lance is discussed in greater detail in *The tactical unit: the lance*, Part I, p. 54ff.

[2] *Gone* or *gonelle* in Old French meant a sleeved tunic reaching the knees (cf. English *gown*).

FULL ARMOUR IN THE 15TH CENTURY

1. Front view: a) crest; b) crown; c) sight; d) ventail; e) cheek-pieces; f) bevor; g) wrapper; h) haute-pièce or pasguard; i) pauldron; j) cuirass rest; k) cuirie; l) cannon of upper arm; m) couter; n) plackart or paunce; o) cannon of forearm; p) gauntlet; q) fauld; r) tasset; s) cuisse; t) side-wing; u) poleyn; v) greave; w) solleret.

2. Back view: a) rondel of the armet; b) spaudler or pauldron (spaudlers did not always overlap at the back); c) back-plate; d) guardreine; e) culet; f) side tasset or flanchard; g) coat of mail.

3. Armet seen in profile. The red line shows the position of the visor when raised, and the outline of the bevor; (x) marks the hole where the plume or crest was attached.

4. Side view of right couter.

5. Side view of left couter. This piece, like the left pauldron, was made larger so as to afford better protection to the side that was most exposed to blows.

6. View of the left poleyn and its side-wing. The suit of armour shown here was copied from an Italian model made around 1450, the period when the forging of suits of armour was at its zenith. These harnesses were all made to measure; a suit for a man of average height (1.60m) would weigh roughly 25 kilos.

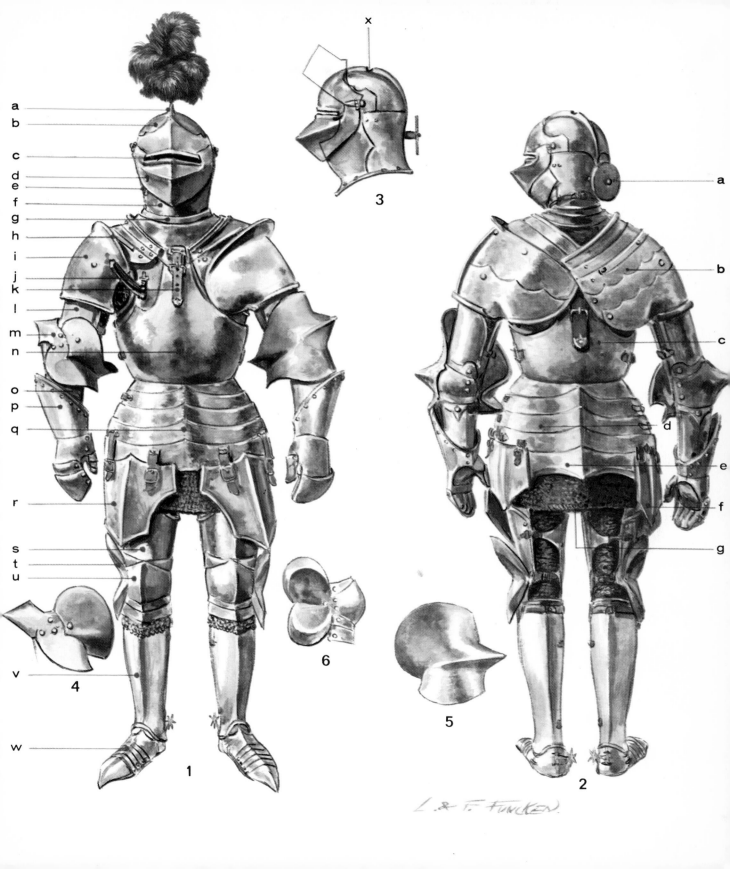

a
b
c
d
e
f
g
h
i
j
k
l
m
n
o
p
q
r
s
t
u
v
w

x

a
b
c
d
e
f
g

1

2

3

4

5

6

L. & F. Funcken.

The development of armour

Rather than present the reader with a text which the many illustrations of armour throughout this book would make superfluous, we have chosen to provide a chronological table tracing the evolution of armour and helmets between the 13th and the 15th centuries.

Date	Development of Armour	Helmet
c.1250	Ailettes first worn on shoulders.	Helm.
c.1300	First reinforcements of steel plates appear on shoulders (spaudlers), knees (poleyns), elbows (couters) and shins (greaves).	Helm.
c.1300	Complete 'gutter-shaped' defence for the arms is worn for the first time, fifty years before it comes into widespread use; the chest is protected by a varying number of curved plates covered with fabric (coat of plates, cuirassine, cuirie, cuirasse).	First bascinets with bulbous or proboscis-shaped visors.

GERMAN ARMOUR OF THE 13TH AND 14TH CENTURIES
1. Standard-bearer of Rudolf of Hapsburg (1298).
2. Knight (1360).
3. Standard-bearer of the Imperial counts of the Rhine (1350).
4. Warrior wearing leg and arm defences made from leather reinforced with iron strips (1360).
5. Warrior wearing a 'steel chest-piece' over his uniform (1360).
6. Note the very rudimentary plates protecting the shins in this figure (1370).
7. Armour made of lames, or thin strips of metal, known as a *Spangenharnisch*; it is worn here in conjunction with a steel 'chest' with its four guard-chains. This armour was normally hidden beneath a surcoat (1350). All the suits of armour pictured here illustrate the transitional stage between mail and full armour. The use of guard-chains was particularly widespread in Germany, as was the wearing of mail, which survived there longer than in other countries. The predilection of the Germans for mail was encouraged by the manufacturing methods of a Nuremberg craftsman called Rudolf, who succeeded in turning out mail of all weights at a very low cost.

Date	Development of Armour	Helmet
c.1350	Emergence of the 'steel chest' with up to four guard-chains for the dagger, sword, shield and helm; arms and legs are by now completely encased in armour.	Helm; the bascinet with aventail and breteche become more widespread; bascinet with face-guard, kettle-hat, sallet.
c.1360	Invention of cuirass rest for supporting the lance when it was being levelled at the opponent.	
c.1370	Full 'white harness' appears for the first time.	'Frog-mouthed' helm; bascinet with suspended visor.
c.1380	First appearance of laminated fauld.	'Hounskull' bascinet, barbute.

GERMAN ARMOUR OF THE 14TH AND 15TH CENTURIES
1. Banner of the Holy Roman Empire. The knight is wearing a suit of armour with a tetrahedral plackart (called a *Kastenbrust* in German).
2. Standard of the cavalry of the Dukes of Bavaria (c.1450). The knight is wearing a sallet with a bevor complete with crest and lambrequin – a very rare sight indeed, as these were normally only found on great helms. 3. Banner of the cavalry of Saxony (c.1430). 4. Banner of Bohemia. 5. Great standard of the Hussite cavalry. 6. Hussite infantry flag. 7. Hussite standard. The goose and the chalice were the emblems of the followers of Jean Hus, fighting under the command of Jean Zizka. 8. Armour designed for combat on foot, with a tonlet and a tetrahedral plackart (c.1450). The cuirass rest for supporting the lance would be superfluous in foot combat, and the fact that it is incorporated here suggests that this suit of armour could be adapted for wearing on horseback simply by removing the tonlet and replacing it with the classic fauld. 9. Infantryman wearing a suit of armour made of overlapping pieces of solid mail (first half of 15th century).

Date	Development of Armour	Helmet
*c.*1395	Tassets worn for the first time.	Great bascinet; war helm no longer in use.
*c.*1410	Corselet armour with laminated fauld worn.	
*c.*1430	Fluting appears on the side-wings of couters and poleyns.	
*c.*1450	Full armour perfected.	Bycocket, armet with vervelles, later superseded by armet with gorget; sallet competes with armet for predominance.
*c.*1460	Short laminated tassets appear.	
*c.*1475	Fluting becomes more extensively used, particularly in Germany; Italy and Germany produce the finest examples of 'Gothic' armour.[1]	The elegantly-shaped sallet comes into general use.

[1] The subsequent development of armour, and its rapid decline, will be discussed in Part 3 of *The Age of Chivalry*.

ENGLISH ARMOUR (i)
13TH, 14TH AND 15TH CENTURIES
1. A warrior wearing a kettle-hat with a bevor, a 'cuirie', or leather cuirass, and metal couters and poleyns (1220). Note the semi-sheathed (quasiguénée) solid mail here and in figs. 3, 5 and 6. 2. The thin strap across the forehead of the warrior in this figure was used to attach the ventail or wrapper of the hauberk, over which the cylindrical helm was placed (1277). 3. and 4. Warriors of 1325. 5. Warrior of 1327. 6. Warrior of 1330. The guard-chain over his left shoulder was for holding his helm when he was not wearing it on his head. 7. Warrior of 1360. 8. Warrior of 1364. 9. Warrior of 1384. 10. Warrior of 1397. 11. Warrior of 1401. 12. and 13. Warriors of 1410.

This plate traces the development of plate armour, which at first was restricted to couters and poleyns protecting the elbows and knees; gradually, however, it came to cover the limbs, and then finally the entire body. Figs. 1–7 are wearing hauberks, while figs. 7–13 are wearing bascinets that have a mail aventail attached to them by means of staples, or vervelles. When going into combat figs. 7–11 would have donned a great helm over the bascinet shown in figs. 3–6. Figs. 7, 9, 10 and 11 are wearing the military belt of the nobility, which only knights were entitled to don; the others, in contrast, are all wearing the baldric. These richly-decorated belts were first adopted in England, and it was there that they survived the longest, only disappearing from use in 1420. (Elsewhere they had ceased to be worn in 1400.)

Full plate armour reached its zenith in the mid-15th century. Only a very few complete suits of armour have survived to this day, and most of them from this period on show in our leading museums are in fact 'composites', i.e., they have been assembled from sections taken from several different suits of armour. Nevertheless they manage to create a more than adequate impression of what these elegant suits of armour must have looked like.

To manufacture a complete suit of armour required considerable experience allied to an exceptional degree of technical skill. Poitiers, Bourges, Paris, Arras, Ghent and many other European towns all gained a reputation for the quality of their craftsmanship, but the great centres of Augsburg in Germany, and Milan in particular, produced a vast number of suits that were highly prized if exorbitantly priced.[1]

Many a gentleman ruined himself financially for the sake of owning a suit of armour bearing the signature of Missaglia, Negroni or Helmschied; these makers, the most famous names of all, belonged to veritable dynasties of 'beaters and furbishers', of *maestri armaoli* and *Plattner*.

While we are mentioning these renowned craftsmen, it would be unjust not to pay tribute to the memory of other equally outstanding masters of the art, men like Hans Grünewalt, Valentin Siebenburger and Wilhelm von Worms of Nuremberg, Conrad Seusenhofer and Adrian Treitz of Innsbrück and the Colmanns of Augsburg. In addition, many suits of armour were produced by unknown craftsmen working in humble workshops right across Western Europe. Although they bear no sign of a stamp or a diemark, these suits testify to the maker's total command of his craft. Anonymous suits of armour of this kind are sometimes looked on with suspicion, but they can be distinguished from counterfeit models by the purity of their lines, their proportions and their 'lifelike' appearance – all qualities which the forger is usually unable to reproduce. In any case a stamp of guarantee or a diemark are easy to copy, and hence do not constitute a guarantee of authenticity on their own; it is unlikely, too, that an expert would be deceived by them.

Most of the suits of armour that we see in museums date from the 16th century and are made in a wide range of

ENGLISH ARMOUR (ii)
14TH AND 15TH CENTURIES

1. Knight in 1413, wearing the Order of the Garter on his left leg (see also figs. 5, 6 and 12). Note the metal plates or lames protecting the area of the armpits in this figure; these were called 'small plates' or 'palettes', and served the same purpose as the breastplate shown in figs. 3, 4, 6 and 8. 2. Warrior of 1420. 3. Warrior of 1414. 4. Warrior of 1425. 5. Warrior of 1416. He is carrying the then late Richard II's banner; it incorporates the coat of arms of his ancestor, Edward the Confessor (a cross pattée), which he occasionally adopted. 6. Warrior of 1419. The collars or necklaces that can be seen on several of the figures often signified allegiance to a certain prince or party – particularly during the Wars of the Roses in the 15th century. 7. Warrior of 1465. 8. Warrior of 1410. 9. Warrior of 1458. 10. Warrior of 1473. 11. Warrior of 1430. 12. Warrior of 1425. 13. Warrior of 1488. 14. Warrior of 1460. 15. Great bascinet (late 14th-early 15th century). It was probably worn by all the warriors in figs. 1–8 and 11–12 (see below).

Note the incredible size of the couters in figs. 9 and 14, which are called 'garde-bras'. It appears that they only reached such exaggerated proportions in England. Most of the figures on this and the previous page have been copied from effigies on tombstones – usually copper engravings done with tremendous care and attention to detail. However, it is disturbing to note the total absence of visors, which implies the use of a cylindrical helm worn over a bascinet in combat. Although tradition has it that this helm was worn at Agincourt in 1415 (and it can still be seen on the tomb of Henry V in Westminster Abbey), in our opinion it seems much more likely that what was in fact worn was the great bascinet with visor shown in fig. 15. The sculptors of the period no doubt wanted to show the features of the dead man and so would have left out the visor of the helmet – which in any case was difficult to render in correct perspective in a way that would be comprehensible to all. The great helm, we should remember, had disappeared from use at the end of the 14th century, and only survived as part of the traditional jousting equipment. It became a complete anachronism worn over full armour, the so-called 'white harness'.

[1] A very ordinary suit of armour would have cost at least 10,000 new French francs.

different sizes. One surprising feature about them is that a man of medium height of our day cannot usually 'get into' an average-sized suit of armour; he generally finds that the cuisses and the greaves protecting the legs, in particular, are too small for him.[1] In the 16th century the saying went that you could always tell a Frenchman by the thinness of his legs.

We have now moved a long way from the image of knights as formidable giants that is so often presented in historical tales. For all that, our ancestors were far from being puny; their physique was more of the wiry, muscular type. The average height of the Latins was 1.6 metres, while the Germanic peoples were markedly taller.

FRENCH ARMOUR OF THE 14TH AND 15TH CENTURIES

1. Man-at-arms wearing a bascinet with a movable ventail in two parts, which could be locked together by means of a turning-pin. The plaited gambeson and leg armour are made of leather (late 14th century).
2. Gendarme from the ordinance companies of Charles VII, carrying the king's personal standard (c.1450). The armour of the horseman and the bards of his mount are both Gothic in style (the same as on the previous page; however at 88 kilos they weigh far more. Here we have a classic example of the hopeless struggle of armour to keep up with the developments in early firearms. Paradoxically this élite body of cavalrymen, who were, in fact the first permanent unit in the French army, were only capable of charging short distances and suffered from lack of manoeuvrability. In addition the prohibitive cost of one of these German suits of armour meant the wearer was reluctant to risk damaging it until it was strictly necessary, with the result that when any action was taken it usually came too late. 3. Knights in marching and ceremonial dress (mid-15th century). The first one is wearing an 'armour-plated' brigandine and a plackart, while the second is dressed in a ceremonial cloak edged with fur called a 'létice'.
4. Banner of Joan of Arc (1430). As the Maid of Orleans was not a knight banneret, strictly speaking she was not entitled to a banner (she was reproved at her trial for failing to observe this rule). The other side of the banner depicts an angel holding out a lily to the Virgin Mary.
5. Personal standards of Louis XI.
6. Banner of France during the reign of Charles VII. 7. Standard of Charles VIII.

[1] The pioneers of military archaeology already noted this fact a century ago.

1

2

3

4

5

6

7

L. & F. Funcken

Armour and the ethics of chivalry

At this point, it would no doubt be useful to consider for a moment the 'moral' aspect of armour and its development.

It is disturbing to note the parallel between the growing decline of chivalry and the successive improvements in armour. 'Is it not strange', wrote Pierre Lacombe,[1] 'that this development in armour, and all the complicated precautions men took to protect their own skin, should occur right at the height of the age of so-called chivalry . . . To my mind, the little infantryman of the present day . . . seems closer to the military ideal . . . than the hulking baron encased in metal and armour. During the baron's time the word 'chivalry' certainly existed, but whether the thing itself did is another matter.'

Clearly we must not generalize about this, and we should refrain from accusing the majority of feudal lords of cowardice – although in the face of the spectacle of their feats of valour the temptation to make subjective judgments is certainly strong. However, it is no less obvious that the protection of a full cuirass gave the wearer a distinct advantage in armed combat and decreased the risks considerably.

A comparison could be drawn between the man-at-arms and the leather-girt American footballer of today. However skilful or brave the latter may be, if he were stripped of his protective clothing he could only go on playing until such time as he had a serious collision with an opponent; in fact, without any protection he would not even survive his period of apprenticeship. However absurd our comparison may appear at first sight, the parallel between the two is nonetheless striking. The footballer's 'armour' is vital to him if he is to practise his violent sport, just as it was indispensable to the martial 'disport' of feudal times. It neither cancels out nor confirms the worth of the wearer.

It is from this point of view that we should consider the real function of armour, and leave it to the champion himself to show us his strength of character and physical bravery.

[1] See Part 1, p. 8.

ITALIAN, SWISS AND GERMAN ARMOUR OF THE 15TH CENTURY
1. Italian armour, 1450, with horse bards dating from the same period; these are, in fact, the oldest known examples of this type of horse armour. The knight's helmet, which illustrates the bascinet in the later stages of its development into the armet, is the Italian *gran bacinetto*. 2. Swiss infantryman wearing armour of the late 15th century; he is carrying the banner of the canton of Unterwald. On his head he has a deep sallet with a restricted sight similar to the one shown in fig. 3. The armour he is wearing was probably taken from the body of an enemy knight killed in battle (the looting of armour was a common practice at the time). Since the battle of Morgarten, in 1315, the arrogant nobility had suffered a series of swinging defeats at the hands of the Swiss infantry, which was made up chiefly of peasants and was to become a model for infantrymen throughout Europe. 3. Italian armour (1480). 4. German armour (1480). Figs 3 and 4 make it easy for the reader to compare the two styles that characterized the magnificent work of the great armourers who produced the armour we nowadays describe as 'Gothic'. 5. Banner of Bologna (1380). 6. Banner of Venice in the 15th century. 7. Banner of Florence in the 15th century. 8. Banner of Berne in the 15th century.

Part III will describe how suits of armour became regarded solely as status symbols. Yet these remarkable works of art were to herald the decline of the suit of armour as a purely protective garment and its eventual disappearance in the face of the armour-piercing bullets of the arquebus.

ARMOUR OF THE LATE 15TH CENTURY

1. Full equestrian armour forged at Landshut in Southern Germany (c.1480). It is decorated with the characteristic fluting of the period. 2. Reconstructed suit of armour dating from the same period as fig 1. It is sometimes attributed to the Missaglia family of Milan, although it is stamped in several places with the mark of Jörg Treytz of Innsbruck and two of his colleagues. The Italian style of armour was characterized by its more rounded lines and its shorter sallet. However there are several examples of suits from both countries that combine the characteristic features of the two styles. 3. German armour of 1480. This is an outstanding example of the work of the famous Helmschmied of Augsburg, the town that was Milan's main rival in the art of forging armour. The German style was characterized by its more angular lines and its frequent use of brass ornamentation. 4. Royal standard of England in the 15th century. It had been the same during the reign of Edward III, in 1339, and was to remain unchanged until the time of Elizabeth I. On her death in 1603 the arms of Ireland and Scotland were added to it. 5. Standard of the Duke of Lancaster, the future King Henry VII, during the Wars of the Roses. 6. Armourer's marks of the 15th century: a) Jörg Treytz of Innsbruck; b) Tomasso Missaglia, of the celebrated Milanese dynasty of armourers; c) Domenico Negroli of Milan; d) guarantee mark of Nuremberg; e) German mark. The fleur-de-lys did not signify French origin, as one might expect, but designated Italian as well as German products.

These costly suits of armour were highly prized in France, and, despite their appearance, were relatively light: the weight a horse had to carry, including armour and rider, was approximately 130 kilos. In comparison, the horse of a cuirassier in 1914 had to carry on average 128 kilos (see *Arms and Uniforms – The First World War* Part 1).

4

5

1

2

3

6

a

b

c

d

e

III INFANTRY OF THE RENAISSANCE

The Swiss

Morgarten

By the late 14th century the short-lived blaze of military glory enjoyed by the communal militias[1] was already beginning to wane. However, there was one small nation with its own formidable infantry force, and that was Switzerland. The very first Swiss infantry had been formed nearly a century before, in 1291, from the confederation of the three Forest Cantons – Uri, Schwyz and Unterwalden – to meet the threat of the Habsburg Empire; sixteen years later, in 1315, it was to brave the might of Austrian chivalry at the pass of Morgarten.

On this occasion Leopold I's[2] cavalry (and this shows their disdain for their Swiss adversaries) was spread out over a distance of more than half a mile when they were rash enough to enter a narrow pass. The 'Alpine shepherds', as the Swiss were known, were lying in wait for the invaders on the heights above and crushed them with an avalanche of rocks and treetrunks. Three quarters of the force of two thousand knights were destroyed and the infantry that had been raised by the Duke at Zug and Zurich fled without further ado.

Sempach

When Leopold, Duke of Austria,[3] mortified by the swingeing defeats his house had suffered in its struggle against the Swiss, took up the cudgels against the Swiss Confederation again in 1386, he found that the nobles of Swabia and Aargau rallied willingly to his cause. Lucerne, Zurich, Glarus, and Zug had now joined the Confederation; however, Berne, which had had its support in 1339 at Laupen in a battle against the feudal aristocracy of the Vaud and Jura, adroitly came up with a host of reasons to prevent it from joining with its saviours on this particular occasion. The Swiss historian, Müller, comments on this episode as follows:

> When we consider the actions of the Bernese at this period, prior to and following the declaration of war, we can commend the skill with which they went about acquiring seignories; however the battle of Sempach must always be a blot on their record of achievements.

This volatile situation finally erupted when a group of young Lucerners became exasperated by the extortionate demands of Hermann Grimm of Grüneberg and carried out a daring 'commando raid' on the town of Rothenburg. Leopold, as it happened, was returning from his victorious campaign in Alsace and he decided there and then to destroy the upstart Confederation. In fact no less than fifty-three declarations of war were issued against it in twelve years.

The Duke and his allies, with an army four thousand strong made up of knights and mercenary footsoldiers, captured the town of Reichensee and massacred its entire population. They next advanced to upper Aargau in order to take Lucerne and the Forest Cantons by surprise while the rebels were still waiting for them outside Zurich. As soon as the Swiss realized their mistake they rushed to the defence of their endangered territories and on 9 July, 1386, took up position in a wood overlooking the lake of Sempach.

SWISS INFANTRY *c.*1500
The Swiss infantry, which came into being at the end of the 14th century at a time when the power of the communal militias of Flanders was on the wane, was eventually to serve as a model for the whole of Europe. The footsoldiers of the confederated cantons revolutionized the tactics of feudal warfare with their square formation, similar to the Greek phalanx, and their three rows of pikes, a reminder of the Roman legion. The Swiss fought as a united and well-disciplined unit. The charge in quick time, for example, which took place in total silence, must have been a particularly impressive sight. Any man who was wounded was forbidden to leave the battlefield, or even to complain of his injuries; anyone who committed an act of cowardice was immediately slain by the man fighting next to him.

The first two standards in the picture (working from left to right) are from Schwyz; the rest come from Nidwald, Uri, and Berne respectively.

---

[1] See captions Part 1, p. 78–80.
[2] Leopold the Glorious of Habsburg (1290–1320).
[3] Leopold III of Habsburg, born in 1351, was the grandson of the Leopold who was defeated at Morgarten. He died at Sempach.

Leopold ordered his knights to dismount and hold their long lances in the rest position – perhaps remembering the lessons of Crécy and Poitiers, or possibly considering it hardly worth while to attack such feeble opposition on horseback.

The contrast between Leopold's men and the Swiss army, which numbered a mere twelve hundred men in all, was striking. The majority of the Swiss were armed with halberds, a weapon which had first been used at Laupen. In this battle it was responsible for bringing down eighty barons and several hundred gendarmes. The Swiss wore no armour at all; as peasant mountain dwellers they had little use for costly and heavy suits of armour. They also made it a point of honour not to carry steel, except on the tip of their weapons.

Their entire uniform consisted of a tight-fitting doublet and chausses, mainly in red 'quartered' with blue, green, or white, worn with a kind of beret made of curly wool and decorated with a plume or feather. The men in the front line of the army carried a piece of wood or bundle of twigs tied to their left arm for protection.

The serried ranks of the feudal army waited for the attack with the raised lances of the first four rows forming an impenetrable wall of spikes. Meanwhile the Baron de Hasenburg, an old and experienced soldier, had sized up the opposition and voiced his fears concerning them. However his doubts were greeted by a storm of protest, and the inevitable punster came up with the taunt, *Hasenburg, Hasenherz!* (literally, hare castle, hare heart).

After a short prayer the Swiss rushed into the attack. Either because of their haste or as a deliberate tactical move they were drawn up in wedge formation to charge the steel wall of the enemy. They literally broke against it in a wave, and lost about sixty Lucerners on the first impact; among the dead was the leader of the Lucerne troops, Petermann de Gundoldingen, an *avoyer*.[1]

It was at this stage in the battle that Arnold Strutthan de Winkelried, from the canton of Unterwalden, sacrificed his life for his fellow-soldiers. Seizing hold of as many lances as he could, in a few seconds he killed enough of the opposing defence to enable his comrades to make a decisive breach in the enemy ranks.[2] The Swiss, handling their halberds with strength and skill, then went on to massacre the opposing knights who were weighed down by their superfluous armour and hindered by their lances, which were too long for hand-to-hand fighting. Terror-stricken and in disarray, they called in panic for their horses, but their squires had already fled as fast as their mounts would carry them.

The defeat turned into a disaster. Leopold fell in the carnage along with most of the noble lords from his army. In an ironic way the vow he had taken was granted, as he had sworn to conquer or die on the soil of his inheritance.

Once again it was the absurd arrogance of the feudal knights that brought about their downfall. The men they were fighting against were battling for their very lives, and for those of their kin. They were comrades bound to one another in a bond of brotherly solidarity, confronting together a ruthless enemy (Leopold's men had even got ready ropes to hang any survivors of the rabble army).

The Confederation, having won its independence from the Habsburgs in the north, went on to consolidate it with the victory of Näfels in 1388. The Swiss army then headed towards the south.

Arbedo

The next target of the Confederation was Valais and the southern side of the Alps; in attacking this region they were challenging the powerful dukes of Savoy and Milan.

---

[1] *Avoyer* was the title given to the two leading magistrates in some Swiss cantons.

[2] In Switzerland Winkelried is as famous as William Tell though he remains practically unknown elsewhere – unlike his almost legendary companion who is renowned all over the world. There exists a victory song sixty-four verses long that mentions Winkelried's sacrifice; it is, incidentally, one of the most interesting examples of the German dialect spoken in Switzerland in the 14th century.

INFANTRY IN THE EARLY 16TH CENTURY
1. Hussite closed wagon (*c.*1420). At the same date as the Swiss adopted the 5.50 metre pike to halt cavalry charges, Jan Zizka devised a barrier constructed of fortress wagons which was to withstand five campaigns by the German feudal armies. 2. Hussite drum. The drum was to go on increasing in size right up until the 17th century. 3. Hussite horseman (*c.*1420). Note the flaps of his boots. 4. Carter (early 16th century). His appearance has remained unchanged for a century. 5. Landsknecht drummer (*c.*1515). 6. Sergeant (*c.*1450). 7. Landsknecht flute-player (*c.*1515). 8. Surgeon setting a fracture (1517).

It was Carmagnola, a condottiere[1] in the service of the Duke of Milan, who in 1422 was entrusted with the task of bringing the Swiss to heel. The wily Italian surprised them at Arbedo, near Bellinzona. The Swiss, with their halberds and shortlances,[2] were unable to withstand the trained cavalry of the *condotta*, who surrounded their enemy and charged them with their long lances held in the rest position.

The Swiss footsoldiers were decimated. The survivors extricated themselves from the battle and withdrew to their mountain homeland.

The birth of the infantry

The Swiss heeded the lesson of Arbedo. Henceforth it was decided that the army should be equipped with 5.85 metres long wooden pikes made of ash which would be capable of piercing a horse's chest before its rider's lance could strike the attacking pikeman. The use of halberds,[3] whose broad hooked heads tended to get entangled and catch on to clothing during close combat, was greatly restricted. Henceforth it was kept as a back-up weapon: the lance would be used to stop the horse, the halberdier then attacking the unhorsed rider.

Shooting weapons in the form of bows and crossbows had been in use for many years; from the late 14th century onwards the 'gunpowder shaft' or hand gun had been part of the equipment of the 'gens de trait' (literally, shooting men). Gradually, with the appearance of the *sclopette* (escopette) and the *Hakenbüchse* (arquebus) around 1450,[4] it finally came to take the place of the bow and arrow.

The Swiss, however, were extremely slow to adopt the use of firearms. After the battle of Granson in 1476 they even went as far as limiting the number of firearms used to fight the Burgundians, who were far more frightened of pikes than of bullets.

The number of arquebusiers employed in the Swiss infantry varied as its military successes began to fall off: in 1476 arquebusiers made up one third of the infantry, in 1480 one tenth. By the beginning of the 16th century they accounted for one quarter of its strength.

Armour

The contempt in which armour had long been held by the Confederation was finally overcome with the perfecting of the firearm. Even then the Swiss held out until 1465 before introducing it, and restricted its use to front-line pikemen only.

At first armour was used to protect the trunk only. However, the tactic which the gendarmes started using in 1501, whereby they 'drew out' the Swiss front line first with crossbow and then with pistol fire, soon forced the Confederation to protect the arms and heads of its soldiers as well.

The decision to sanction the wearing of armour presented no problems as regards equipment, as the Swiss arsenals were filled to bursting with suits of armour that had been captured from the enemy. The only difficulty was choosing which one to wear.

As head protection the Swiss soldier wore the elegantly-shaped sallet or a simple skullpiece concealed beneath his beret.[5]

WEAPONS USED TO UNHORSE THE ENEMY
Special weapons were needed to capture wealthy fighting men, in return for whom hefty ransoms could be obtained. (In 1388 the chronicler Froissart denounced this calculated 'taking of hostages', which is becoming fashionable again today.) Some examples of these weapons can be found on p. 51 of Part 1. The introduction of smooth, impermeable armour meant that the practitioners of this lucrative trade had to devise special sprung forks known as *désarconneurs*. The Germans, in particular, used these ingenious *Fangeisen* to great effect, and many examples of them are still to be seen in German museums today.

The figure in the foreground is holding a combined 4-barrelled hand gun and mace known as a *Schiessprügel* in German. The two riders are wearing suits of Maximilian armour dating from around 1515 to 1520; one is a 'costume' type and the other is fluted.

Some of the more observant readers among you may have been struck by the rather anachronistic garb worn by the footsoldiers in the illustration. For example, the sallet-cum-bevor worn by the figure in the top right of the picture and the Gothic cuirass of the figure in the centre are both thirty to forty years old. Even more surprising is the combination of a medieval mail aventail and the most up-to-date model of infantryman's armour. Obviously there were frequent instances of pieces of equipment being used to arm several generations of fighting men in succession.

[1] *Condottiere* (leader) means a mercenary commander. A true 'war entrepreneur' from the 14th century onwards, he hired himself out with his *condotta* to the countless nobles that ruled the patchwork of Italian states.
[2] The Swiss lance was at that period only 2.60 to 2.90 metres long – equivalent in length to the halberd.
[3] See the chapter on staff weapons, Part 3.
[4] See the chapter on firearms, Part 3.
[5] See p. 57, fig. 2.

Internecine wars

The Swiss did not learn their military skills overnight; these evolved slowly over long centuries, among a body of citizens who were not subject to any feudal obligation of military service. In addition the practices of civic law meant that every Swiss had learnt how to handle a weapon of his own choice long before the outbreak of internal conflicts that preceded the confederation of the three original cantons.

During the first thirty years of the 15th century the members of the Confederation were occupied in tearing each other apart. Zurich appealed to Austria for aid in 1440; then in 1443 France provided support in the shape of 30,000 *écorcheurs* under the command of the future King Louis XI. The peace treaty was signed thanks to the efforts of outside arbitrators, and the quarrelling factions were reunited in 1450, ready to meet Austria in 1468.

Granson

Sigismund of Tyrol had been forced by a chronic shortage of funds to give up the landgrave of Alsace, together with some Rhenish towns, as security for a loan of 50,000 florins from the wealthy Charles the Bold. This provided an opportunity for Charles to reunite the two sections of his territory, namely Burgundy and Flanders. In invading the duchy of Lorraine, which bordered on Alsace, Duke Charles was taking the first steps towards reconstituting the former kingdom of Lotharingia, of which it was his dearest ambition to be crowned king. He 'had so many grand schemes', writes Philippe de Commines,[1] 'that he had not time enough to see them completed; in any case, they were almost impossible, for not even half of Europe would have been enough to satisfy him'.

Louis XI of France saw an opportunity here to rid himself of a formidable foe. He had little difficulty in winning over young René de Vaudémont[2] to his plan for recapturing Lorraine. He then payed off Sigismund's debts, and pressured the Swiss into going to war.

In 1473 Colmar, Mulhouse, Sélestat, Strasburg, and Basel were already united in a defence league; a year later they were joined by Sigismund, who was now reconciled with the Swiss. It was the Swiss, in fact, who led the attack by capturing several towns, among them Granson, Orbe, Jougne, and Morat.

Charles now joined the fight at the head of a powerful army of 40,000 men supported by the finest artillery available. The duke's treasure – his jewels, finery and gold and silver plate – brought up the rear; the plate alone weighed 12,237.5 kilos.

Yverdon fell first, followed by Granson in 1476; its garrison, which was reduced to 412 men, was ruthlessly massacred. On 2 March the reinforcements, which had arrived too late, ran into an army of 30,000 Burgundians out to engage them in battle. Charles thought he would make short work of these 20,000 peasants; they knew nothing at all about the art of war, yet had dared to challenge a strategist like himself.

The Burgundian heavy cavalry, drawn up in wedge formation, opened the attack with a charge that broke up on the pikes of the Swiss vanguard, who stood unwavering. Then the harsh notes of the 'bull of Uri' and the 'cow of Unterwalden' rang out – those 'grand and glorious' horns which, it was claimed, had been presented to the Swiss long ago by Pepin and Charlemagne. Their sound signalled the arrival of the main body of the Confederation army and the mere sight of it was enough to throw terror into the hearts of the Burgundian infantry. A counter-attack by Charles' cavalry was swept aside by the sheer drive of the Swiss, who were drawn up in square formation. The mighty Burgundian army took to its heels with losses of only 400 men, leaving behind a vast quantity of spoils[3] for the enemy.

---

[1] 1447 to 1511. Author of the *Mémoires* chronicling the reigns of Louis XI and Charles VIII of France.

[2] 1451 to 1508. He was the future René II, who became Duke of Lorraine in 1473.

[3] The booty consisted of 600 banners, 420 cannons, 800 arquesbuses, 1500 chariots, 10,000 horses – and literally tons of gold and silver, which the Swiss sold as if it was copper and pewter. There was also the huge diamond belonging to the Grand Mogul, which sold for an écu.

ROYAL BODYGUARDS
1. Gentleman from the reign of Francis I carrying a *bec-de-corbin* (1520). 2. Mounted cranequineer of the Guard of Francis I (1520). 3 and 4. Scottish archers of the Guard of Henri II (1559). They are wearing 'Albanian' felt hats. 5 and 6. A Scottish and a French archer of the Guard of Francis I (1520). 7 and 8. A French and a Scottish archer of the Guard of Henri III (1580). 9. Standard of Francis I (1515–1547). 10. Standard of Henri II (1547–1559).

Charles was unable to stem the tide of panic sweeping his forces and was forced to flee to Jougne in the pass of Jura. His jester made the following apt comment on this move: 'Oh, Sire, now we have been well and truly Hannibalized!'

Morat

The Burgundian army was miraculously reformed within a month, and its strength was reckoned at 35,000 soldiers drawn from Picardy, England, Lombardy, the Vaud, Savoy, Burgundy and South Italy. In June 1476 this force set up camp outside the walls of Morat. The town's tiny garrison of 2,000 men put up a stubborn resistance while waiting for a relieving army of Swiss to arrive. These troops, now reinforced by their allies from Alsace and Lorraine, were led by young René de Vaudémont, the duke without a duchy.

This army of 22,200 footsoldiers and 1800 cavalry[1] left Berne at ten o'clock in the evening and arrived outside Morat in time for matins.

Duke Charles faced the Swiss ranks with his men divided up but covered by solid artillery entrenchments. The first Swiss attack was successfully repulsed. However the duke was a poor general who made it a point of honour 'not to deign to move'; thus he failed to take advantage of this initial success by counter-attacking, and the Swiss vanguard broke through on the right flank. Then, in a sudden thrust forward, they captured the Burgundian artillery and turned it on the enemy.

The battle lasted for three hours. Charles the Bold tried vainly to save the day but was completely bewildered by the tactical skill of the enemy battalions. His cavalry managed to drive Duke René's horsemen from the field, but was forced to fall back under the onslaught of Swiss pikes that rushed in to fill the breach. Morat's garrison made a vigorous sally and the rearguard of the Confederation army

began to turn back the Burgundian army. The latter was left with only one possible escape route – the lake.

A terrible massacre followed the Burgundian defeat. The majority of the eight to ten thousand dead were slain in cold blood as they floundered in the mud. The bones of the vanquished formed a hideous memorial on the site of the actual battle.[2]

Nancy

The events at Morat won the Swiss universal acclaim and renown. However, for Charles the Bold they meant the ruin of his reputation as a military leader; in addition, they led to his vassals finally erupting into rebellion when he tried to claim a quarter of their wealth in order to raise a new army of 40,000 men.

In the end the despotic Charles, much to his disgust, had difficulty in raising an army of even 6,000 men with which to avenge himself for his defeat. He went and laid siege to Nancy, where the meagre garrison of English and Burgundian sol-

---

[1] These figures are, as always, approximate. The Confederation army may have been slightly superior in numbers to Burgundians, except in artillery. Philippe de Commines mentions a figure of 31,000 men, which includes 4,000 cavalry. The Italians reckoned the strength of the Burgundians at 20,000 to 22,000 men while Burgundian writers put forward figures of 28,000 to 30,000.

[2] This memorial remained for three centuries until 1798 when, paradoxically enough, it was destroyed by the French battalions of the Yonne and Côte d'Or which were part of the invading Revolutionary armies.

THE PIKEMAN IN THE 16TH CENTURY
1. Italian pikeman (1500). In place of the cap shown here he sometimes wore a barbute (see Part I, p. 29, figs. 2 to 6) or a simple bowl-shaped skullpiece. 2. Swiss pikeman (1510). The suit of three quarter armour he is wearing is typical of those worn by infantrymen at this period. It consists of a breastplate and backpiece, with an additional pair of small side-plates that fasten over the ribs and are attached to the backpiece by hinges. 3. Swiss pikeman (1530). He is wearing a suit of armour captured from the enemy in battle. He has taken off the spaudlers, the cuirass rest (which is useless to him), and the leg pieces so as to have as much freedom of movement as possible. His pike is fitted with a deflecting disc or brise-perspective (literally, a 'view-interrupter'). 4. German pikeman (1555). The sword he is wearing is an Italian schiavone. This was the period when knee-breeches reached their most grotesque proportions. 5. Pikeman's armour (1570). The corselet was to remain in use until the mid-17th century, always with a certain amount of decoration. By the time it fell into disuse, however, its quality was so poor that the tassets were made in one piece, while the lamellae and rivets were purely decorative and were stamped out in one process from a piece of sheet metal that was about as impervious as cardboard! 6. Pikeman's armour (1582). By now the corselet has lost its spaudlers, its 'stumps', and 'peapod'-shaped busc (see fig. 5). The standard of workmanship of the cabasset and the suit of armour in this figure already point to the rapid decline of the armourer and his craft.

diers, unable to hold out any longer, had just opened its gates to Duke René II on the 6 October, 1476.

René did not have enough troops to wage a pitched battle, and so went off to seek the support of the Swiss. The very harsh winter took an even greater toll of the besiegers than the besieged. Four hundred Burgundians died of cold on Christmas Eve alone. Charles refused to abandon the siege, despite the hostility of his men, and swore he would celebrate Twelfth Night as conqueror of Nancy.

On 5 January, 1477 Duke René suddenly reappeared at the head of a Swiss vanguard made up of 7,000 footsoldiers and 2,000 cavalry, all of them crack troops; they had been joined en route by detachments of troops from Alsace, France, and Lorraine. A little to the rear of them marched ten thousand Swiss. The Duke of Burgundy, ignoring the advice of his captains, decided to give these 'villeins' and 'drunkards' the reception they deserved. Not even the treachery of his most trusted friend, the Neapolitan condottiere Campo Basso, could persuade him to change his mind.

The battle began with Duke René and his cavalry making a bold head-on charge against the enemy artillery. This move was successfully followed up by a massive infantry attack which broke through the Burgundians' right wing. The left wing was suffering a similar fate when the Nancy garrison sallied out to join in the massacre.

Split up, scattered, and pursued in all directions, the army of the Grand Duke was in ruins. Four hundred fleeing soldiers tried to escape by the bridge of Bouxières, but the renegade Campo Basso drove them back towards the Swiss army.

Charles, for his part, had fought like a lion. In the general debacle he was dragged towards the marshy ground around the pool of Saint-Jean. It was here, on 7 January, that a young Italian page in the service of the noble family of the Colonnas identified the naked body of his master. His head had been

split open from the ear to the mouth, and his thighs and the base of his spine had been stabbed by the terrible blows of the halberd.[1]

Customs

The Swiss army had a tradition of kneeling in prayer before the start of a battle. It was this custom, in fact, that led the Burgundians to think for a moment at Granson that their enemy was asking for mercy.

When the Swiss were actually fighting, on the other hand, they did not bother with the rules of chivalry observed by the nobility – who, it should be emphasized, were alone in observing them. As far as the Swiss were concerned it was a question of no ransom, and no prisoners taken. This harsh treatment was meted out with equal severity to any man on their own side who was guilty of cowardice, desertion, or evading conscription.

Serving a foreign power

The victories won by the Confederation army caused an enormous stir throughout Europe, and soon their services as soldiers were being sought.

The first monarch to employ the Swiss was Louis XI of France. As early as 1453 he enlisted 6,000 of them for his planned conquest of the Franche-Comté. When peace was declared in 1480 Louis employed them as instructors for his new militia; this was to produce the famous 'Picardy bands', the forerunner of the French infantry.

By the end of the century the Swiss were to be found serving in Italy, fighting both for and against Venice, and aiding the rivals of the duchy of Milan.

---

[1] As often happens in the case of famous personages, the claim was made that the mutilated corpse was not in fact that of the duke. This has been put forward as a probability by some historians; however, several individuals closely connected with the despotic duke were able to officially identify the body by some old scars, the teeth, and a ring left behind because the stone was too small to appeal to the men who plundered the body. The traitor Campo Basso, who probably knew more than anyone about his master's death, gave 'guidance' to those carrying out inquiries.

THE HALBERDIER IN THE 16TH CENTURY
1. German halberdier (1520). 2. Halberdier's armour (1520). The breastplate with the rounded base shown here is typical of the period from around 1510 to 1515. 3. Swiss infantry captain (1525). The armour he is wearing is a Maximilian suit of extremely fine quality dating from 1510 to 1515. 4. German halberdiers (1500 and 1510). They are typical examples of what the original landsknechts looked like. 5. Halberdier (1546). He is wearing a 'bishop's mantle' made of mail. 6. German halberdier (1560). 7. Swiss halberdier (1584). 8. Spanish halberdier (1572). They were recruited in Belgium and French Flanders and in Hainhault, and were considered the most formidable infantrymen of their day.

They also served in the army of Pope Julian II, where from 1506 onwards they were to provide the famous papal guard – *pro custodia palatii nostrii* (for the protection of our palace).

Charles VIII, Louis XII, and Francis I of France all enlisted large numbers of Swiss in their armies. Louis XII employed 24,000 of them in 1500; Francis I, perhaps for reasons of economy, tried to use men from the district of Gruyère, but surprisingly enough these turned out to be very poor soldiers. The success of the Swiss had inspired a sense of arrogance in them, and with it an exaggerated confidence in their ability to win battles without any cavalry or artillery support. This attitude was to lead to some unpleasant shocks for the Confederation army, like, for example, their defeats at Marignano in 1515 and Biccocca in 1522.

Crises also arose when two contingents of Swiss soldiers found themselves fighting one another in opposite camps, as at Novara in 1500. Here they abandoned the Duke of Milan, Ludovic Sforza, leaving him entirely at the mercy of Louis XII of France. The Swiss were difficult and temperamental soldiers, often refusing to fight over uneven ground, or demanding higher wages. They meant what they said, too – hence the proverb, 'No money, no Swiss'. However, in the words of another saying, 'If the Swiss aren't for you, then they're against you'. Consequently many a ruler was forced to enlist them.

The development of a national infantry was repeatedly interrupted by the demands of war; moreover, any villein who became a soldier passed from being a bondsman to a free man and could no longer be reclaimed by his master once peace was restored. Despite this, in 1522 Henri II already had two national battalions of 25 to 28,000 men in his army, compared with a third battalion of 'Germans' containing 7 to 8,000 men.

However, the heirs of Morgarten were finally eclipsed, firstly by the increasing use of artillery and then by their imitators, the landsknechts, and similar bodies in other national armies. Although they fought as bravely as ever, the fact that they were no longer unique diminished the importance of the role they played on the battlefield.

¹ See *Arms and Uniforms – The Lace Wars.*

The Swiss continued to serve France honourably up until the reign of Louis Philippe in 1830.[1] They also fought for England from 1690 to 1856, and went to war for Austria in the 15th and 16th centuries, and then again in the 18th; they served in the armies of Spain from 1515 to 1823, of Holland from 1676 to 1828, and of Prussia, Russia, and Italy. All in all, it is an astonishing record of achievements.

The landsknechts

The landsknechts were originally valets who accompanied a knight and carried out the various duties of a domestic servant, ostler and soldier. Here, as was the case elsewhere, the demands of war led to their numbers increasing until eventually they were formed into troops of varying strengths which went to make up the German infantry. At the end of the 15th century the Emperor Maximilian I created an infantry modelled on the lines of the notorious Swiss infantry. Its members were called *Landsknechte*, from *Land* meaning flat countryside in German, and *Knecht*, meaning a servant; in other words, they were 'men of the plain' in contrast to the Swiss 'men of the mountains'.

The fame of this new infantry soon spread throughout the whole of Europe. Every ruler wanted to have them in his service, more especially after the swingeing defeats suffered by the Swiss at Marignano and Pavia in 1515 and 1525, which badly damaged their reputation.

THE BUCKLER
1. A nobleman armed for a judicial duel (mid-15th century). His equipment consists of a tournament target and helmet. Full traditional armour was also worn in tournaments. 2. Battle target (1435). It has a notch for supporting a lance. 3. Rondache with a hook for breaking lances (1520). 4. Hand-held target (*c.*1500). 5. Fencer with a rondache in the shape of a rooftile (1560). 6. *Bras à parer* (early 16th century). 7. Judicial duel between the German commoners (1443). The special combat shields were used in fencing. 8. Lantern rondache (early 16th century). 9. Spanish soldier with an adarga (1540). 10. Pistol-cum-rondache (1550). There are several examples of this odd contraption still in existence today. 11. As above; this inside view shows the breech and obturator. 12. Soldier carrying a rondache (early 17th century). 13. *Bras armé* (early 16th century). 14. *Bras à parer* (early 16th century). 15. Gentleman officer of the company of Henri III with a dress rondache (1580).

1

2

3

4

5

6

7

8

9

10

11

12

13

14

15

L. & F. Funcken

In France the long pike used by these new mercenaries led to the corruption of their name from *Lands* to *lans*, the French word for a lance – hence the French spelling of the word as lansquenet. This interpretation of the word passed into popular parlance in Germany itself, where *Lands* was replaced by the German word for a lance (*Lanz*) to coin the term *Lanzknecht*. The English in their turn coined the word *lance-knight* and in so doing accidentally elevated a peasant soldier to the status of a knight! Not for the first time semantics took something of a beating, but at least the national pride of everyone concerned was saved.

The organization of the infantry

George von Frundsberg, known as 'the father of the landsknechts', was the man responsible for setting up the new-style infantry based on the Swiss model that was to be the instrument of military power of Habsburg Austria and the Holy Roman Empire. Germany at this time was meaningless as a political entity, split up as it was between a host of petty sovereigns, bishoprics, and independent towns. Young men in search of adventure, impoverished petty nobles, and the inevitable pack of gallows birds all enlisted under the orders of high-born colonels, or even simple commoners, which was remarkable for the time.

These colonels, or *Obersten*, commanded ten to sixteen companies known as *Fähnlein*; each of these contained 400 men under the command of a captain, or *Hauptmann*, assisted by his lieutenants and ensigns (*Fähnriche*). This hierarchy laid down the foundations of the modern military system, and these 'bands' were to form the first properly constituted regiments at the end of Charles V's reign. Each was made up of eight ensigns of 300 men.

A considerable number of landsknechts were recruited from the Rhine area, although the most famous of them came from Swabia.

Wherever the landsknechts served they provided the solid backbone of the infantry, and they became the model for the first national regiments to be formed.

Weapons

The weapon most commonly used by the landsknechts was the pike. At three to four metres long it was shorter than the Swiss pike, but it was held by the end of the shaft in order to give the maximum possible reach. The landsknecht would charge, holding his body in a characteristic hunched posture, and then stab his opponent. The landsknecht held his lance low, in contrast to the Swiss and French who held their lance at chest height, gripping it near the middle of the shaft so as to distribute the weight more evenly.[1]

The use of the double matchlock and light wheel-lock arquebus seems to have been far more widespread among the landsknechts than the Swiss, as was the wearing of the cuirass and the distinctive *Sturmhaube* or burgonet. The broad-bladed short sword known as a *Katzbalger* (cat gutter) or *lansquenette* corresponded to the *Schweizerdegen* used by the Swiss.

Traditions

The landsknechts would pray before the start of every battle, after which they would throw a handful of dust in the air or kiss the ground. However, this pious custom did not stop them from

INFANTRY SWORDSMEN
1. Espadon (second half of the 16th century). The two hooks below the handle were used to 'shorten' the guard at certain points in the fighting; they could also be used to parry backhanded blows and to increase the effectiveness of forward thrusts. The wavy blade was supposed to inflict more damaging wounds. 2. Espadon (late 11th century). 3. Second half of the 15th century. 4. Late 15th century. 5. 1500. 6. Mid-16th century. The sword shown here is the Italian *spadone a due mani*. 7. Mid-16th century. 8. Note the S-shaped quillons (1520). 9. Double-pay soldier in full armour (1520). 10. Scottish soldier with his claymore or *claidheamh-mor* (literally, great sword) (16th century). The two-handed sword was normally carried slung over the back like a guitar, as shown in the illustration. 11. Double-pay soldier (1580). Veterans who fought in the front line and wore armour received double pay – hence the name.

Much has been written about the risks these swordsmen caused their fellow-soldiers as they brandished their deadly weapons in battle. It appears, however, that they only intervened in exceptional cases, and in fact accounted for only a very small percentage of the infantry. A drawing by Holbein the Younger shows only one swordsman for every thirty or so pikemen and halberdiers (see 'Tactics').

[1] This applied to infantry combat, of course.

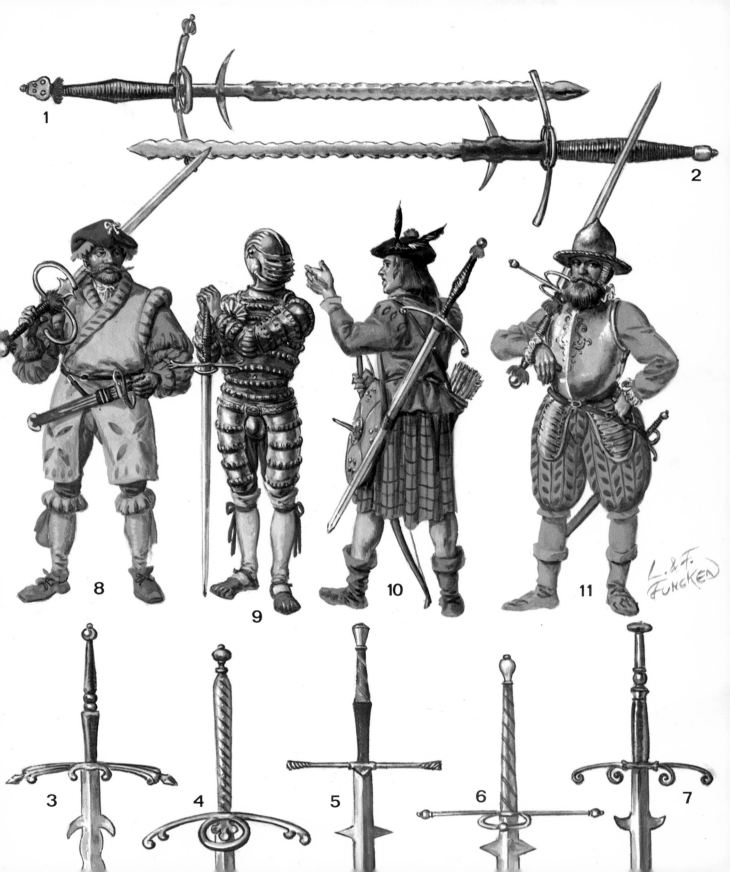

serving both the Protestant and the Catholic causes with equal fervour.

The landsknechts were of wholly German origin but they were joined by adventurers from every nation – Low Germans from Limburg, Luxemburg, and the German-speaking cantons across the Meuse, for example. All used to join in singing the following words:

Wir haben gar keine Sorgen
Wohl um das römische Reich

The Holy Roman Empire
Doesn't worry us much

Consequently they were shown no mercy by the landsknechts of Charles V's army.

The terrible cruelty of these 'wicked tearaways' is no legend. Their wild behaviour was enough to frighten the devil himself, or so they claimed. In the course of the Italian Wars, the Dutch Wars, and the Wars of Religion the landsknechts committed unspeakable atrocities. In Belgium, twelve Belgian landsknechts were executed on the orders of their Spanish commanders as a punishment for crimes they had carried out against their compatriots.

The practice of hiring landsknecht mercenaries died out at the end of the 16th century. In Germany itself they disappeared with the outbreak of the Thirty Years War in 1618.

The development of national infantries

The less than flattering terms generally used to refer to footsoldiers tell us a good deal about the low regard they were held in by feudal society. Although, as we have seen, the emancipation of the communes led to the formation of militias that were often formidable as fighting units, they were also reluctant to accept discipline or to fight for any interests other than their own.

The free archers

It was Charles VII who was responsible for setting up the *free archers*[1] in France. This body of infantry soon became the butt of the nobility's ridicule and gained the nickname of *francs-taupins* (literally, free moles); this was a reference to their proverbial cowardice which led them to hide themselves away in holes, just like a mole. It should be said that these unfortunate wretches did not enjoy the privilege of being ransomable, and so had no way of saving their lives other than by fleeing. This 'collection of moles' rebelled on one or two occasions and was eventually disbanded.

In 1466 Louis XI re-established twenty-eight companies of 500 *free archers*, each of which was made up of guisarmiers, pikemen, and arbalesters (crossbowmen). However, the only major battle they took part in, Guingate in 1479, earned them their dismissal a year later on the grounds of lack of discipline. They were brought back in 1485 by Charles VIII but were disbanded for good in 1508, under Louis XII.

In the 15th century the equipment of a *free archer* consisted of a sallet worn with a jacket lined with twenty-five to thirty thicknesses of cloth, or a brigandine lined with small metal plates.

Regular infantry

Because Swiss mercenaries were so expensive to hire, the kings of France decided to raise regular bands of infantry. These were most often made up of Gascons 'as human as leopards', and Bretons who dressed 'scoundrel-fashion' in slashed and ragged breeches. Many of them had a fleur-de-lys branded on their shoulder, or hid a missing ear under their shock of hair (it had been cut off by the hangman). It is hardly surprising that these disruptive troops earned themselves the nickname of louts or hustlers.

ARQUESBUSIERS AND MUSKETEERS
1. English arquebusier (1520). 2. Landsknecht arquebusier (1520). 3. Arquebusier (1530). At this period the arquebus had no firing mechanism and the match was still operated by hand. 4. Landsknecht arquebusier (1560). 5. French musketeer (1585). 6. French musketeer (1590). 7. Musketeer (1580).
Note the pitchfork device carried by the musketeer to help support the heavy musket while he took aim.

[1] For information on the cavalry of this corps, see Part I, p. 126, figs 9 and 10.

Louis XII on occasion managed to raise the general standard of these bands by subjecting them to strict discipline. The nobility, and in particular the 'broken lances' – ruined gendarmes known as 'lanspessades' – did not consider it beneath them to take on this new infantry, as the need for it was growing increasingly apparent.[1] In fact since the reign of the previous monarch it had been generally acknowledged that 'mounted men cannot easily accomplish any great feat without footsoldiers'. Nevertheless, Louis XII took only 13,000 infantrymen with him on his Italian campaign, in comparison with no less than 29,000 cavalry.

Bands from 'up north' and 'down south'

Initially Francis I preferred to use foreign mercenaries rather than the regular infantry, despite the fact that it was already gaining a reputation because of the famous 'Piedmont bands'. These had been trained by a Spanish renegade called Navarro along the lines of the *soldados* in his own country. The escalation of hostilities led in 1521 to the creation of four major military districts – Champagne, Picardy, Piedmont and Guyenne.

The bands from Picardy and Champagne, known as 'the bands from up north', fought in the north, while Piedmont and Guyenne, 'the bands from down south', defended the southern part of the country. Thus the first four regiments of French infantry were established.

The legionaries

In 1523 the continuing struggle against Charles V forced a return to the old custom of levying *free archers* in every French parish. Francis I indulged his taste for things classical by transforming his newly-formed regiments into seven 'legions' of 6,000 legionaries each. They were divided up as follows:

First legion – Normandy
Second legion – Brittany
Third legion – Picardy
Fourth legion – Languedoc
Fifth legion – Guyenne
Sixth legion – Burgundy, Champagne, and Nivernais
Seventh legion – Dauphiné, Auvergne, and Lyonnais.

Each legion was split up into six 'cohorts', which were in turn divided into twelve ensigns with an equal number of captains; these were to be under the command of a colonel[2] (the first time the rank was used). The arquebusiers accounted for 12,000 of the double-pay men in the army.

However the legionaries were only a match for their namesakes when it came to pillaging and looting. They were undisciplined and cowardly, and caused nothing but trouble.

Henri II tried to re-establish the legions in 1588, but they disappeared in the general confusion of the Wars of Religion. The old bands[3] with their *corselets* (pikemen and halberdiers) and arquebusiers in their traditional morions or bonnets, now numbered only 15,000 men.[4]

In 1560 Charles IX set up the first properly constituted 'regiments' and gave each leader the title of *mestre de camp* (camp master);[5] the title of colonel was reserved for commanders of foreign regiments. The reorganization carried out in 1569 established the institutions of the regiments of the French Guard on a permanent basis; these were drawn from Picardy, Piedmont, Champagne, and Navarre.

Henri IV retained them as the backbone of his infantry which was otherwise rather unevenly constituted as regards both the number and strength of its ensigns. In time of war, for instance, there were

---

[1] Both Bayard and Montluc were prepared to lead this infantry.
[2] At that time the rank was called *coronnel* or *coronel*.
[3] Only Champagne, Picardy, and Piedmont remained active in peace time.
[4] Exact details on the strength of the legions are given in the chapters on helmets, firearms, etc.
[5] Regiments raised in war time took the name of their *mestre de camp*.

INFANTRY MUSICIANS
1. 1520. 2 and 3. 1572. 4 to 6. 1580. 7. Cuirassine. This was a concealed cuirass which was often worn underneath the *bosse de polichinelle* (Punch's humpback); the hump was also used to hold all manner of odd articles. The transverse flute, which originally came from the East, was introduced into Europe by way of Byzantium. It was commonly used by the Swiss and by the German landsknechts, and was often dubbed the *Schweyser Pfeiff* or *flauste d'Allemaigne*. There were four instruments in all in the flute family, each with a different pitch.

barely more than 200 men to an ensign instead of the regulation 300.

Incidentally, Spain and Italy, like England, Sweden, and Austria, had by this date already had their own standing national armies for some time.

The royal guard

Philip Augustus was the first to recruit 'Scots guards' as part of his 'mass guards' or 'sergeants at arms'. From 1453 onwards they acted as the sole royal bodyguard.

Louis XI added a company of a hundred gentlemen of the royal household who were known by the title of *bec-de-corbin*. He was also responsible for setting up the *cent-suisses* in 1475. Louis XII added a further company to the 'hundred gentlemen', who were henceforth known as *la grande Garde du corps* (the Grand Bodyguard).

During the reign of Francis I the gentlemen of the *bec de corbin*, who now numbered 200, served in battle as cranequineers in the horse archers of the Guard. Henri IV, however, thought it wiser to pay off the 'old diehards', and added a company of light horse to his guard. In 1563, his predecessor Charles IX had created the famous regiment of the French Guard. From 1515 onwards Francis I had a personal bodyguard of sixty French archers and twenty-four Scots archers.

The famous English Yeomen of the Guard had been safeguarding Henry VIII since 1509. Before his time only sergeants at arms were responsible for guarding the life of the English sovereign – a situation which lasted from the reign of Richard the Lionheart until that of Richard III (1189 to 1485).

The buckler

The term 'buckler' is derived from the Vulgar Latin *bucularium*, *buculerius* or *bucularius*, or possibly from the old German word *Buckel*, meaning a bump.

Whatever its origin, the buckler was considered a vital part of a fighting man's equipment from the dawn of antiquity. Large versions of the buckler were usually hung round the neck by the 'guiche' or 'guige'; in addition, all bucklers were fitted with a pair of straps, one for the arm and one for the fist, which were known as 'enarmes'.

The development of the buckler

1230 The buckler becomes shorter; at this date examples measuring more than a metre in length are rare (see Part I, pp 19 and 43).

1260 The evolution of plate armour means the ecu[1] can be made lighter and its size reduced to an equilateral triangle about 60 cm square. From the late 13th to early 15th centuries ecus are richly and freely emblazoned in a style that is clearly visible from a distance (see Part I, pp 25 and 27).

Early 14th century: The ecu is reduced even further in size but is now longer than it is wide.

1320 to 1350 As the Honourable Ordinary known as the chief becomes more commonly used in heraldry, the sides of the top quarter of the ecu gradually become parallel and vertical; this means that the rectangular outline of the chief can be more clearly represented (see the coats of arms in the heraldry illustrations in Part I).

1360 to 1380 Although the ecu undergoes no obvious change during this period, its sides acquire a more pronounced curve. At the same time it frequently increases in size (see Part I, pp 27 and 35). It is worn high on the chest, supported by a guige, leaving the left hand free to hold the reins.

Mid-fourteenth century: The tip of the ecu is now concave and points forward. The dexter cannon often has a V-shaped indentation to support the shaft of the lance (see p. 49). This feature is

---

[1] The ecu (from the Latin *scutum*, a shield) was the buckler used by the men-at-arms in the Middle Ages. The symbols and emblems painted on it were originally ecus taken from coats of arms; from the time of the reign of Saint Louis these emblems were depicted on certain coins which subsequently came to be known as *écus*. Interestingly, a European conference held at Bremen in July 1978 decided to set up a European currency based on the *écu*!

THE CENT-SUISSES
1 and 2. *Cent-Souysses* of the Guard of Louis XII (1507). Their uniform was described as 'party-coloured' or 'quartered'. The shoes in fig. 2 were called *escafignons*. 3. A Cent-Suisse (1520). 4. Cent-Suisses captain during the reign of Francis I (1520). 5. Under Henri II (1559). 6. Under Charles IX (1571). 7. Under Henri III (1580).

1

2

3

4

5

6

7

L & F
FUNCKEN

frequently found in conjunction with a rib running the length of the shield, a kind of heavily marked 'fold'. At this period the towns of Paris, Rouen, Nuremberg, Vienna, and Ghent all had first-rate craftsmen producing such shields.

Mid-fifteenth century: The ecu is now worn only at tournaments and jousts, where its place is later taken by the target. Improvements in armour henceforth made the buckler more of an encumbrance than an aid to its wearer.

The pavis

The pavis, formerly known as the 'pavais' or 'pavart', was the shield generally carried by foot-soldiers (see p. 31, and Part I, pp 77, 93, 95 and 97).

It fell into disuse in western Europe in the late 15th century, but continued in use in eastern Europe until the 17th century.

The rondache

The rondache, a type of small round buckler, was known as a 'rouele' in the 12th and 13th centuries. It was carried by mounted troops in a few rare instances in the south of France; north of the Loire it was fairly uncommon, while in the East and in eastern Europe, on the other hand, it was extensively used.

The true rondache, which was made of metal of *cuir bouilli*, made its appearance in France in the 13th century. It was no bigger than 31 cm in diameter and was used only by the 'common herd', or soldiers on foot. An even smaller version called the 'boce' or 'hand roundel' (see Part I, pp 53 and 83) was known as a *rotellino* in Italy. Around the mid-16th century fencing rondaches with a hook for parrying the opponent's blade were being produced.

By the end of the 16th century the rondache had been withdrawn from use in almost every army in Europe, except for Holland, where it continued in use among the 'rondachiers' of the infantry until the early 17th century.

The target

The target is featured heavily in the illustrations to all parts of this work. For a long time it was regarded by early poets as interchangeable with the ecu, and even small bucklers were called 'round targes'.

In the 16th century small targets in the shape of squares, rectangles, or trapeziums, which were known as 'hand targets', were used in fencing.

The adarga

The *adarga* was a typically Spanish weapon of ancient Moorish origin. It was made of layers of lined leather which were stuck together before being stitched in place.

The adarga was particularly widely used by the Iberian cavalry. It enjoyed the rare privilege of outlasting all its rivals – in fact it was still in use in Mexico in the late 19th century.

ENGLISH, SCOTTISH AND IRISH TROOPS
1. Provincial gentleman (1548). He is wearing a mixture of modern armour and obsolete garments such as the hauberk and the habergeon (see fig. 7). 2. Yeoman of the mounted escort of the Guard during the reign of Elizabeth I (1575). 3 and 4. Yeomen of the Guard (1520 and 1575). The initials ER did not appear until 1570, although Elizabeth acceded to the throne in 1558. 5. Officer of the Guard (1520). 6. Scottish light-cavalryman (1580). 7. Scottish infantryman (c.1580). 8. Irish chieftain during the reign of Elizabeth I.

IV CAVALRY OF THE RENAISSANCE

The French *compagnies d'ordonnance*

For a long time feudal cavalry, particularly in France, had reigned almost unchallenged as the mainstay of the army, as the nobility jealously guarded its right to defend its heritage and its privileges.

The once high and mighty lords who had been ruined by the Hundred Years War now found themselves obliged to hire out their services by enlisting in the new-style *compagnies d'ordonnance* of Charles VII (see p. 55, and Part I, p. 56). And even if this desire to serve in the front line was often forced upon the nobility by dire financial hardship, it nevertheless does them great credit that they were prepared to fight.

Many a knight sacrificed his last remaining *écus* in order to kit himself out with the finest weapons and horse available. In this way he stood the best chance of being selected by the royal commissioners to enter the élite body of the *compagnies de la grande ordonnance*. Here, in the year 1439, the monthly pay for one lance consisting of a man-at-arms and five subalterns was thirty pounds. Anyone who was turned down by these companies could find a place in the *compagnies de petite ordonnance* set up in 1449; these, significantly enough, were also known as the *compagnies de petite solde* ('small-pay' companies).

Not even the poorest knight would have taken it into his head to enlist in the rank and file – this was only fit for 'commoners and men of low estate'.

Theoretically each of the fifteen *compagnies d'ordonnance* contained 100 men-at-arms, who were all lance commanders, and 500 cavalrymen. The cavalry were less heavily armed and were divided up into the following groups: 100 pages, 300 archers, and 100 custrels. The gendarme had four horses

maintained by the State, the page had one, and the archer and the custrel had two apiece, making a total of 900 horses in each company.

The men-at-arms were clad in armour from head to foot, as were their mounts; they fought independently as heavy cavalry. They were addressed as *maître* (master) to distinguish them from their subordinates; in fact this title was to remain in use in the French cavalry for many years.[1] The rest of the troops operated as light cavalry; they were accompanied by a varying number of unpaid 'volunteers' who served in the army while they waited for a vacant place to arise.

The number of men in a lance tended to vary. Louis XI fixed its strength at five cavalrymen; then in 1489 Louis XII decreed it should be seven men, increasing it to eight in 1513. In the reign of Francis I this figure fell to six men in 1530, then in 1550, under Henri II, it fluctuated between six and eight. At times, however, it was as high as ten or twelve. In 1561, in the reign of Charles IX, the total complement of sixty-five companies amounted to only 2,590 men, and only four companies still had the full complement of 100 cavalrymen originally laid down; most of the others had only thirty-three cavalrymen apiece. During the Wars of Religion, which lasted from 1562 to 1570, the average strength of a company was about thirty-four men, and these were of an increasingly poor standard.

The gendarmerie was the weakest section in the entire army because of general apathy and a high desertion rate. Indeed it became so altered in character from its original conception that many

THE SWISS CAVALRY
The Swiss cavalry were comparatively small in size and their chief role was to reconnoitre the route for the main body of the Confederacy army and to provide cover for the artillery and flanks. In the illustration opposite they are shown on the morning of the battle of Nancy, which took place on 5th January 1477. The battle began with the first massed charge ever by Swiss cavalry. Most of these Swiss cavalrymen have nothing at all in common with the men-at-arms who traditionally made up the cavalry in other armies. The Swiss were mounted footsoldiers who preferred to fight with the halberd rather than the long lance. They usually carried a scimitar-type sabre instead of a sword. The footsoldier in the picture is wearing a 'loden' cloak. These are often referred to as if they were an invention of our modern textile industry; in fact they date back to the first centuries of our age.

[1] See *Arms and Uniforms – The Lace Wars.*

L & F. Funcken

commoners simply took a title when they joined up, and the meanest scoundrel capable of staying on a horse could call himself a gentleman.

Henri III was forced to send for the reiters from across the Rhine, and he imported twelve regiments of these troops. Under Henri IV the cavalry underwent what amounted to a purge, as a result of which its second-rate troops were eliminated and first-class Huguenot *maîtres* were introduced. The last *compagnies d'ordonnance* to be worthy of the name were downgraded by the Edict of Nantes in 1600; the expulsion of all gendarmes who had only served in time of civil war further reduced the companies to a minimal strength.

Equipment

The armour and equipment of a man-at-arms and his mount had, of course, changed with the fashion of the times, and there were few *maîtres* so impoverished that they would make do with an old-fashioned suit of armour.

Between 1461 and 1483, during the reign of Louis XI, a total ban was imposed on the wearing of velvet and silk by members of the *compagnies d'ordonnance*, and this temporarily ruled out all extravagant forms of dress for them. Quite a few excessively clothes-conscious gentlemen had their pay docked for daring to infringe the royal prohibition. When all this finery was banned from the armies of the French king its sole outlet became the forces of the Duke of Burgundy, where there was ample scope for indulging even the most expensive tastes.

The thick crest-plumes brought back by Louis XII from the Italian Wars gave way to the finer plumes worn during the reign of Francis I. At the same time harness for horses became lighter with the abolition in the ordinance of 1534 of the bard protecting the mane. Nevertheless it took many years before cavalrymen finally gave up wearing the heavy, cumbersome pieces of armour that took so long to fit into place. Eventually the full equipment was reserved for parades (*montres*) when the royal commissioners carried out their inspection.[1]

[1] See the chapter on the horse and its harness, Part 3.
[2] They reigned continuously from 1405 to 1419, 1419 to 1467, and 1467 to 1477.
[3] See Part I, p. 53.

The Burgundian *compagnies d'ordonnance*

John the Fearless, Philip the Good, and Charles the Bold[2] all learned to their cost how much the lack of an army that was disciplined, well-trained, and (most important of all) permanent, could jeopardize their political ambitions.

In an edict dated 31 December 1470 Charles took steps to establish his own *compagnies d'ordonnance*. The strength of these troops was first of all fixed at 1,000 men, then later the number rose to 1,250. In 1473 the *compagnie* or *bande d'ordonnance* was made up of 100 'lances', each of which consisted of a man-at-arms, a squire, a custrel, three archers, and three *gens de trait* on foot.[3] The only difference between this and the French lance was that the leader in the Burgundian lance was not called *maître* (master) but *condotier* (leader).

The company was divided up into four squadrons of twenty-five men-at-arms; each squadron was in turn split up into four divisions of six men-at-arms.

REITERS
1. Cavalryman's armour (1540). 2. Medium-quality armour (1580). 3. Poor quality armour (1560). 4. Cavalryman's armour with a closed burgonet (1580). The growing tendency of the long thigh-pieces to be jointed over the abdomen heralds the approach of the 17th century and the shape armour was ultimately to take; in contrast, the pasguards and convex breastplate are a continuation of older features. 5. Light cavalryman's armour; it has a cuirass rest for the lance. The demi-brassards shown in this figure and in figs. 2 and 3 were called 'stumps'. 6. Reiter (1540). These German light cavalrymen were responsible for introducing the wheel-lock pistol into the cavalry armoury; this meant that gauntlets with jointed fingers had to be re-introduced so that the weapon could be properly handled. The gauntlets in fig. 1 are mittens. The practice of covering most of the surface of the armour with a thick coat of black paint meant that suits cost less, as they no longer had to be polished and many of the imperfections in the metal were hidden. It also made them far easier to maintain. The finest-quality suits of armour were not painted, however, but blackened by heat.
The reiters, who were variously nicknamed 'Black Coats', 'Black Harnesses', 'Black Devils', or 'Painted Devils', had a liking for both black and white armour. All the models shown here weighed around 12 kilos, including the weight of the burgonet. Note, however, that this type of armour was also very common among light cavalry (with or without a cuirass rest) as well as among infantry.

The remaining man-at-arms was the leader of the lance. When the company was on the march the 300 archers split up into four squadrons of seventy-five men each. Last of all, the infantry made up a company of 300 fighting men which was divided up into three *centenies* of 100 men. Each *centenie* was under the command of a *centenier*, and was further split into three *trentenies*. Each *trentenie* was led by a *trentenier*.

In addition to these groups there was a troop of unpaid volunteers who could take the fighting strength of the company to as many as 1,500 men. This, not surprisingly, caused a great deal of confusion and made it impossible to establish the precise number of soldiers taking part in any one battle from the figures quoted by the chronicles of the period. The chronicles gave the strength of armies in numbers of 'lances', which contained, as we know, not ten men but any number between ten and fifteen. When this method of reckoning was applied to 200 or 300 'lances', estimations of numbers of troops involved could be out by several hundred. Thus it is impossible to get any accurate figures for the strength of the troops involved in any one particular battle, especially as the practice of taking on volunteers was common.

The Burgundian *bandes* or *compagnies d'ordonnance* certainly appear to have been of a higher standard than their French counterparts. Not only was discipline stricter in the Burgundian ranks, but there were far fewer high-ranking lords, who always tended to be restless and independent.

Equipment

The uniform worn by the *condotiers* was quite dazzling. It was almost identical to the costume of the French *maîtres*, though far richer with its *journades*, *huques*, and *mantelines*[1] made of velvet, silk, satin, and cloth of gold.

As may well be imagined, Charles the Bold was one of the more dazzlingly dressed knights among this gorgeous band of soldiers. He wore military hats made of solid gold and aventails made of gold mail. His swords, belts, and harness were richly studded

with precious stones and pearls. Unfortunately bravura in matters of dress is no guarantee of bravura of spirit, and the whole of Charles's dashing cavalry simply melted away like snow in its three encounters with the Swiss rank and file.

The Austrian *compagnies d'ordonnance*

In 1477 the Emperor Maximilian went to take possession of the fine estates that had fallen to him in the dowry of Mary of Burgundy, the daughter of Charles the Bold. However, on arriving there all he found were the remnants of an army in complete disarray; in addition the provinces had deprived their young monarch of his rights by refusing to return to the old feudal traditions of military service.

Although the *bandes d'ordonnance*, the famous 'legions of Mars', were reduced to a skeletal force, they had not yet been paid off. Maximilian kept them on, at the same time reducing their number to fifty men-at-arms, fifty horse archers, and fifty foot archers; he also placed a captain, not a condotier, at their head. Thus the companies continued to exist in law, although they were never again brought together or employed as a fighting unit.

In 1522 Charles V fixed the strength of the cavalry at eight companies containing fifty men-at-arms and one hundred archers apiece. New bands known as *bandes de crue* (supplementary bands) were added as the needs of war dictated; however, they never became fully merged with the cavalry as such. The *compagnies d'ordonnance* from the regions 'up north' continued to be the training ground in the art of war for members of the nobility, who were even

---

[1] A *journade* was a loose tabard with slashed sleeves. A *huque* was a type of long loose robe. A *manteline* was a dress uniform similar to the *journade*.

LIGHT CAVALRY (i)
1. Mounted crossbowmen (1540). He is wearing a triple-crested burgonet. 2. Argoulet (1560). The argoulets originally came from Spain; they became known as carabins when they began using a shorter weapon (an escopette one metre long) around 1590. The name argoulet comes from Argolis, a region in Greece; the carabins took their name from the Italian province of Calabria. 3. Mounted arquebusier (1590). 4. Pistoleer (1560). 5. German light-cavalryman wearing three-quarter armour (mid-16th century). The 'Hungarian' or 'Oriental' burgonet shown here was typically German in style. 6. Mounted arquebusier, also known as a *ferentario* (c.1590).

admitted into the rank of the humble archer.[1] Every soldier in these companies was a subject of Charles V and came originally from the Low Countries.

The strength of the *bandes d'ordonnance* was increased in 1545 to nineteen companies, then in 1547 it was reduced once more to fifteen. Each *bande d'ordonnance* contained ten lances, a lance at this period being made up of five cavalrymen – a man-at-arms, a page, a custrel, and two archers. Hence a single company had fifty men, plus a captain, a lieutenant, an ensign-bearer, a guidon, a captain of archers, one or perhaps two trumpeters, and a chaplain. The system of division into squadrons and chambers introduced by Charles the Bold was retained.

As for the infantry, it was attached to the *bandes d'ordonnances* for administrative purposes, though when the army was on the move it formed a separate unit under the command of its own leaders.

Equipment

A man-at-arms wore the armour of the period below a 'saye' or a 'full sayon'. These had short sleeves and a thick skirt with heavy folds, or else simply a skirt on its own which was known as a 'demi-saye'. Archers, counting as light horse, wore the demi-cuirass and carried 'the trusty espieu' or the 'hackbut'.

All the monarchs descended from Charles V's line who reigned between 1555 and 1700 (Philip II, III and IV, and Charles II) recognized the value of the *bandes d'ordonnance* as an institution and maintained them as generously as possible. During the period we are specifically concerned with, this superb cavalry fought against France from 1520 to 1559, then on the side of the League in 1567 and 1568. Later they fought at Arques in 1589, and in many other subsequent battles.

The condotta

The multiplicity of petty states and principalities that divided up Italy following the wars between the Guelfs and the Ghibellines on the one hand, and the Papacy and the Empire on the other, all employed mercenaries. The advent of the condottieri was first heralded by the Catalans in the 14th century; their company of almugavars[2] under the command of the *capdil* (a Catalan word meaning leader or guide) fought in Aragon, Catalonia, Italy and Byzantium. However, there were marked differences between the Catalan almugavars and the Italian *condotta*, which was regional in character.

The names of the most famous condottieri are well known, as are the often tragic events of their careers. Piccinino, Vitelli, Vigate, Carmagnola were all to be denied the peaceful end enjoyed by the most renowned condottiere of them all, Bartolomeo Colleoni – the same Colleoni who was immortalized in the equestrian statue by Verrochio in Venice, although he never won an outstanding victory. We tend to forget that their forerunners were Germans (men like Urslingen, Hanneken, or Baumgarten), or English (notably the Hawkwood brothers). The year 1379 saw the appearance of the first great Italian condottieri, Alberico di Barbiano and his company of St George.

The word 'condottiere' never fails to conjure up the clash of epic confrontations and the din of fierce battles. And yet these conflicts nearly always ended

ESTRADIOTS AND GENITORS
1. Estradiot carrying a captured Huguenot standard (*c.*1570).
2. Moorish genitor. These soldiers served in the Spanish army, where they were the equivalent of the French and Italian 'stradiots'. The weapons they traditionally carried were the scimitar and the light *jineta* (a type of lance). According to some sources, however, their name did not derive from the word *jineta* but from the Spanish jennets they took to war with them. 3 to 5. Estradiots (early 15th century). The notch in their shields (known as 'Bohemian' shields, incidentally) was not used for aiming the lance, as is often claimed, but for observing the enemy during battles. In any case the lance, which was extremely light, was held at arm's length, Oriental-fashion, like an assegai. It could measure up to three metres in length.

The estradiots (from the Greek *stratiôtês*, meaning a soldier) were mercenaries who had emigrated to Italy from their native Balkans. Once they enlisted in the armies of Charles VIII of France at the time of his Naples campaign in 1495. The 'stradiots', 'Corvats' (Croats), or 'Albanians', as they were usually called, were completely wiped out at the battle of Coutras in 1587, during the Wars of Religion. They were fighting in the army of Henri III, commanded by the Duke de Joyeuse, which was defeated by the Protestant troops of Henri de Bourbon, the future Henri IV of France.

---

[1] The term 'archer' still survived, even though the bow had not been used as a weapon for many years.
[2] From the Arabic *al-moughâvar*, meaning 'he who carries out raids'.

with little blood being spilt, and sometimes without a single soldier being wounded. The condottiere fought a 'clean' war, using caution and deliberate lack of haste; he tended to resort to diplomacy and *combinazione* (intrigue) rather than the brutal 'dirty' methods of the Swiss and Germans. He never forgot what a valuable investment his men were; in many cases he had even paid for their weapons and horses.

The number of banners in a *condotta*, which was led by a captain, tended to vary. Each banner was under the command of a *bannererius* or constable, and brought together twenty-five 'lances'. Twenty 'lances' made up a 'squadron'; ten 'lances' constituted an ensign, which was led by a 'decurion'. A 'post' comprised five 'lances' in the charge of a corporal.

The tactical unit of the lance itself was composed of a man-at-arms together with his squire and his page. There were few infantrymen, but these could attach themselves to the company. They were known as *fanti* – the origin of the modern French word for a footsoldier, *fantassin*.

Light cavalry

The 9th century saw the first appearance of light cavalry with the introduction of mounted archers and arbalesters (crossbowmen). From the end of the century onwards they faced competition from soldiers firing 'gunpowder shafts' (*traits à poudre*). We show several of the latter in these three volumes.

Light horse

It was the example of the archers in the *bandes d'ordonnance* that inspired the setting up of separate bodies of élite companies known as light horse. Many would-be archers who could not find the position they wanted turned to this fighting unit.

The arms and armour worn by these troops were always lighter than the equipment carried by the men-at-arms and gendarmes of the heavy cavalry. The light horse were less expensive to maintain and equip, and the horses they rode tended to be smaller; as a result their ranks began to swell. They were sometimes called 'sallets', and were divided into units of 100 to 250 men, known as 'cornets'. They were also called *chevalseurs* or *chevaucheurs* until

their present-day title of light horse became established.

Mounted arquebusiers

In France mounted arquebusiers were attached to the light horse and gendarmes in small units of ten to fifty men. An edict issued by Francis I and dated 1534 stipulated that they should carry the following weapons: a small arquebus measuring 0.81 to 1.07 metres which was to be carried in a case of *cuir bouilli* that hung from the right pommel, and a mace on the left. A sword completed this equipment.

Dragoons, carabins, and argoulets

The *argoulets* are the oldest of these three 'specialist' fighting men. They were archers or arbalesters under Louis XI, then in the 16th century they fought with the light arquebus, rapidly gaining the nickname *croque-moutons* (sheep-eaters) – as well as the contempt of the rest of the army. They continued in existence until the reign of Charles IX.

The first troops of dragoon-lancers and dragoon-arquebusiers were formed in Germany at the end of

CUIRASSIERS
1. Cuirassier wearing a cuirass with 'crayfish' thigh-pieces. The additional breastplate formed a double cuirass known as a 'habergeois'. The extra piece made up to a certain extent for the poor quality of this munitions armour, which was mass produced at the lowest possible cost. A suit like this weighed no more than 12 kilos. 2. This figure shows the removable culet being fitted. The thigh-pieces were hung in place in exactly the same way (see fig. 1). 3. Apart from the fact that a cuirassier did not carry a lance, the only things that distinguished him from a lancer were his horse (which was less expensive) and his weapons (a heavy sword, plus pistols of a larger calibre). 4. 'Cuirassier' armour (*c.*1595). Apart from the fine chiselwork decorating it, its polished finish alone tells us it is far superior in quality to the munitions armour shown in figs. 1 to 3. This particular suit would weigh around 30 kilos.

Together with lancers, cuirassiers (who were still known as 'corasses' or 'corassiers' at the beginning of the 17th century) made up the heavy cavalry or gendarmerie of the army. Lancers began decreasing in number from 1560 onwards because of a scarcity of good horses, inadequate wages, and a consequent lack of training. The 'crayfish' armour shown here is frequently (and inaccurately) called *demi-armure* or half armour (*halber Harnisch*), whereas in fact only the greaves for the shins are missing. In English it is known as three-quarter armour or cuirassier's armour, while in Italian it is called *armatura da corazza*.

the 16th century. In France the term was occasionally used to mean a mounted arquebusier.

The carabin, first mentioned in texts during the reign of Henry II, was the equivalent of the Spanish *argoulet*. The name 'carabin' was originally 'calabrin' (these soldiers came from the Calabria region), and it gave its name in turn to the modern 'carbine'. It is most likely, however, that the carabin used an escopette measuring at least 1.17 metres in length. This weapon had a rifled[1] barrel, and was formidable on account of its accuracy and power.

In France, at any rate, mounted arquebusiers (who were commoners) were only entrusted with minor duties and were traditionally given the most fatigues to do. They never enjoyed the prestige of the light or heavy cavalry, who were recruited from the ranks of the nobility.

The estradiots

The estradiots, who were in effect 15th-century Cossacks, had been known of in France from the time of the battle of Fornova (1494). They were variously known as 'Albanians', 'stradiots', or 'estradiots' (from the Greek *stratiôtês*, meaning a soldier); according to Commines, 'They were all Greeks and came from places held by the Venetians in the Morea and around Duras.[2] They were dressed like Turks, infantrymen and cavalrymen alike, except for their heads where they did not wear the piece of cloth known as a toliban (turban)'.

In addition to wearing a padded kaftan, the estradiots ensured protection against arquebus fire by carrying the first chapter of the Gospel of St John into battle with them. The rather feeble protection afforded by Holy Writ was supplemented first by mail gloves, then steel gloves, and eventually by cuirasses and cabassets.

These tough cavalrymen, who traditionally wore a high-crowned felt hat known as an 'Albanian', were paid a ducat by the Venetians for every Frenchman they killed. Louis XII enlisted 2,000 of these mercenaries, of whom Jean Marot wrote:

'They ride so fast that it seems as if a tempest bears them along', (*Voyage de Venise*). The estradiots ceased to be employed during the reign of Henri IV.

The reiters

The *reiters* (cavalrymen) who came from Germany, were initially recruited by the *Ritter* (knight) from among his serfs. The serf was emancipated in accordance with a ritual inspired by old Germanic initiation ceremonies; he then became a *Meister* (cavalry master) – a kind of squire banneret. Each successful candidate was allotted a valet who was chosen from those remaining serfs.[3]

From about the time of the 15th century the reiter companies belonging to the famous 'black bands'[4] began to gain a certain notoriety. The services of these mercenaries were enlisted by both France and Spain, particularly during the period of the Wars of Religion. The weapon they used, the wheel-lock pistol, was still comparatively new. It achieved spectacular results against the traditional gendarmerie, who were still reluctant to carry any arms other than the lance and the sword.

Some writers have claimed that the gendarmerie broke through the reiter lines on more than one occasion. However, La Noue, the most reliable and best-placed observer among the chroniclers,

LIGHT CAVALRY (ii)

1. German dragoon-lancer (1600). Together with the dragoon-arquebusier shown in fig. 4 he formed a kind of mixed cavalry which operated in small units in Germany. 2. Hungarian hussar (1600). As well as being armed with lance and sword he is carrying a *hegyestör*: this was a combination of a pike and a sword which was designed for attacking armoured cavalry. (See also the plates on swords). The *hegyestör* was the equivalent of the old *branc* of Western Europe which is shown in Part I of this work.) 3. Mounted arquebusier, sometimes called a bandolier or bandoulier (*Bandolierreiter* in German). He is armed with a wheel-lock arquebus. The picture shows him with his complete *fourniment*, or equipment, consisting of a bag of bullets, a key to the wheel-lock and two flasks containing priming powder (in the smaller one) and charge. The weapon was attached to a bandoleer by a ring that slid along a metal rod. The name 'bandoleer' was later to be applied to the shoulder-strap holding the ready-primed charges used by infantry arquebusiers and musketeers (see the appropriate plates). The cuirass is cut away at the shoulders so that the wearer can aim his weapon accurately. 4. Mounted dragoon-arquebusier (*c.*1600). He is armed with a matchlock arquebus and is carrying the same equipment (apart from the key) as the arquebusier in fig. 3. The weapon could only be loaded by the method shown in this figure.

---

[1] See the rifled weapons in the chapter on firearms, Part 3.

[2] Durrës (Durazzo in Italian) was an Albanian port.

[3] These valets are believed to have developed into the landsknechts when the reiters left for service abroad in the 15th century.

[4] This rather sinister nickname quite simply derived from the emblematic colour of the German Huguenots.

declares the opposite to be true in his *Discours politiques et militaires* (1585). Another chronicler, Brantôme, tells us the reiters were 'armed to the teeth and had plenty of pistols' – hence their names, 'pistoleers' or 'pistolled devils'.

The reiters would form up in large squadrons of between 500 and over 1,000 men, then charge in ranks twenty to thirty deep. During the attack each row of troops would fire off their pistols in rapid succession and then return immediately to the rear of their squadron. This manoeuvre was called the 'snail' or 'carousel'. The squadron was divided up into 'cornets', or companies commanded by a *Rittmeister*. The majority of recruits came from Brunswick, Saxony and the Rhine Palatinate.

The 'black devils' would only go into action if they were well enough paid. They received a premium on enlistment known as *Laufgeld*, then an allowance while on the march called *Aufreisegeld*; finally, once they had arrived at their destination, they received their regular wages, known as *monstre*.

The profession of the *barbouillé*, or *chaffouré*, as these reiters were also called, was so profitable that many young Frenchmen of noble birth were sent to learn German in families related to a *Rittmeister* by marriage so they would have a better chance of enlisting in a squadron. 'Since all the money in France was going to pay reiters, every parent hoped to see his son chosen in the levies of reiters'.

The reiters fought at Renty in 1554, and by 1558, under Henri II, they numbered as many as 7,000 men. From 1562 to 1569 they fought in both the Huguenot and the Royalist camps. However, 1587 was to prove a fateful year for them: they were virtually wiped out in a battle at Auneau, near Chartres. The castle moats were piled high with the helmets and armour of the slain, and for two centuries afterwards peasants in the area would come to dig for the metal they needed to repair their farm implements in this 'iron mine'.

Cuirassiers and lancers

The corasses, who later were known as cuyrasses and eventually as cuirassiers, were formed in the mid-16th century. It was, in effect, a bastard type of cavalry that was established in an attempt to halt the gradual decline of the heavy cavalry brought about by losses in men-at-arms and a shortage of suitable mounts. Many gentlemen who had been ruined by a succession of wars were unable to re-equip themselves as they would have liked, and well-trained horses were practically impossible to find.

As for lancers, we might question whether they could still be considered a viable fighting force at this period. The increasing firepower of the infantry must have discouraged many a great cavalry leader.[1] Even the superb companies of the *ordonnance* gendarmerie had lost much of their force since the time of Henri II. The practice of charging at the trot, which had been adopted as a means of overcoming the shortage of adequate horses, reduced the effectiveness of the lance to such an extent that La Noue could write: 'The pistol is capable of buckling defensive weapons, but the lance is not. It is nothing short of a miracle when someone is killed by a lance' (*Quinzième Discours*, 1590).

In the Austrian Netherlands at the end of the 16th century the cavalrymen of the *compagnies d'ordonnance* traded in their title of 'gendarme' for that of 'lancer'. At the same period in France the only true lancers still in existence were to be found in the troops of the League with their Spanish and Italian mercenaries.

In 1618 Walhausen[2] wrote: 'The corasse is an invention of our time that came into being 50 or 60 years ago when there began to be a shortage of lancers in France and the Netherlands; not enough men could be found and so corasses had to be used in their stead . . . If you take away from the lancer his lance and his solid mount and give him a smaller horse that is no good at all in a sudden clash with the enemy, then you have a corassier'.

LIGHT CAVALRY (iii)
1. Light-cavalryman (1550). 2. Mounted arquebusier. He is wearing a bandoleer holding separate charges primed and ready for use (1600). 3. Light-cavalryman (1550). 4. Light-cavalryman (1550). The rondels protecting his armpits were still in existence a century after they were first introduced. 5. Arquebusier wearing a mandilla, a kind of dalmatic robe with sleeves that was borrowed, oddly enough, from the lackey's uniform. This fashion was all the rage throughout Europe from 1570 to 1580. The mandilla was worn underneath the spandlers, while the sleeves usually hung free.

[1] A Spanish proverb of the time went as follows: 'Once the mount is slain, then the rider is as good as dead'. The horse was the main target that was aimed at.
[2] *L'Art militaire à cheval*.

V SLAVS and ORIENTALS

Scale armour made of solid links had been worn by the Persians since the time of the Achmenid dynasty (550 to 330 BC). It was also used in making horse caparisons of burnished bronze.

Ring mail made its appearance much later, during the period of the Sassanid dynasty (between AD 226 and 651). It was first used in making aventails and surcoats similar to those worn by our own ancestors;[1] however, it was reinforced by gutter-shaped leg and arm pieces made of burnished bronze. Rounded helmets were introduced during the same period; around AD 900 a more pointed spherical ornament began to be worn on the crown. Later on, body armour made of distinctive square plaques called *char-aïna* (four mirrors) was introduced, along with a type of helmet with a fitted nosepiece known as a *kulah-khud*.

The wearing of this type of armour spread from India throughout the whole of the Near East under the influence of the conquering Mongol tribes. The Muslims decorated theirs with delicate arabesques and quotations from the Koran, which were initially written in Kufic lettering, and later in cursive script. They rigorously avoided depicting the human form, as this was forbidden by the Koran.

Full armour itself never really existed outside Western Europe. However, the Turks devised a lighter version of it known as 'jazerant', or, more accurately, *djezireh* (an island), which was made of tiny steel plaques joined together by interlinked mail. The actual coat of mail itself was called *gâdir* (a word meaning 'pond'); hence the *djezireh* was meant to represent islands floating in a pool of water.

Every Eastern country as far as the German and Austrian borders took up using oriental weapons and armour, though not without a slight modification of style involving, naturally enough, the removal of any Islamic features. In Austria itself there were great lords who did not consider it

beneath their dignity to wear the superb plumed harnesses, modelled on the style of the janissaries, which were fashionable in Hungary at that period.

Further afield, in lands where the Danubian principalities (the future modern Rumania) fought a fierce battle against the Turks throughout the 15th century, the cuirassed cavalry of the *pantzirs* of the guard of Stephen the Great wore jazerant and an onion-shaped helmet.

The Russians

In the vast and distant lands of Russia that remained barbarian for so long, the only battle harness worn was the oriental type. Some tribes of the Soviet republics in the extreme south-east continued wearing it until 1940 – an incredible but significant fact.

Like the 'mirror' body armour of the Orientals, jazerant, or mail reinforced with plaques, was reserved for the élite. Also worn was a bizarre-looking helmet called a *misourka*; this consisted of a saucer shape that protected the skull and a tube of mail that was slipped over the head. A square hole cut away at the front left room for the nose and mouth. There was no vision slit – the warrior simply had to peer through the mail. A circular piece of

RUSSIANS AND HUNGARIANS
1. Hungarian hussar (16th century). 2. Russian cavalryman (16th century). Note the whip he is holding, which no horseman would be seen without. It is held in place by a strap which goes round his little finger: the corresponding finger of the left hand could be slipped through a loop in the reins when the rider wanted to use his bow. 3. Hungarian heavy cavalryman (late 16th century). His armour is Turkish in origin, and is a superb example of the 'jazerant' style which was worn throughout the East from earliest times. It was gradually perfected over the centuries in the same way as Western armour. 4. Russian footsoldier (16th century). His armour mainly consists of a habergeon known as a *badiana* reinforced by a plate over the abdomen. His thighs and knees are protected by jazerant armour. The weapon he is carrying is a doloire dating from the end of the 16th century, known as a *berdych* in Russia and a *berdiche* or *bardiche* in France.
Russian helmets: 5. Helmet belonging to Prince Yaroslav (early 13th century). The mail aventail and the 'face' are no longer extant. This is the oldest known example of a Russian helmet, and is made of iron covered in brass and decorated with gold plates. 6. Byzantine *chapel de fer* or kettle-hat (13th century). 7. Helmet with visor (15th century).

---

[1] A great quantity of these mail garments must obviously have been brought back to Europe by the Crusaders at a time when we had almost forgotten the difficult skill of manufacturing it.

jazerant was frequently worn to reinforce and protect the contours of the skull. The most common form of buckler carried was a round shield known as a *kalka*.

In winter the Russian soldier would don his quilted greatcoat. This was similar in style to the kaftan which was worn in the cavalry instead of mail – mail being expensive and probably only rarely found.

Only feudatories and free men could serve in the army; originally they received no pay at all, then, in the 16th century, they were paid a wage in return for their services. This period marked the first appearance of the Russian standing army which in 1584 had a strength of 15,000 cavalrymen; these could be reinforced, if the need arose, by 65,000 mounted soldiers. Each regiment, or *polk*, was commanded by a *golova* (a head). The Russian soldier led an extremely frugal existence and always carried with him his rations of crushed millet and 4.5 kilograms of salt pork plus a little salt, mixed with pepper in the case of the better off.

As a fighting body the Russians were badly trained and undisciplined, and lacked staying power. If the first furious charge turned out to be a failure, they would turn tail. As there were virtually no rewards or honours to speak of, they had no incentive to commit feats of valour. Yet one especially shrewd English chronicler of the 16th century foresaw what the Russians could achieve with a proper military formation. His judgement has since been amply confirmed.

For a long time the Russians used the same tactics as the Tartars, which consisted of sudden charges and abrupt withdrawals. The first tentative appearance of infantry came as late as the beginning of the 16th century, and it was 1550 before Tsar Ivan IV created the first regiments of strelitzes (marksmen). In 1586 there were 12,000 of these troops fighting on foot and on horseback together with an infantry of foreign mercenaries 8,500 strong. Artillery was introduced during the early years of the 16th century but was never entirely effective; the guns themselves were cast on the spot by Italians or Germans.

At the end of the century the Russians used a bizarre kind of wall on wheels in a battle against Polish troops. It was nearly 10 kilometres long, and consisted of a row of wooden blockhouse-shaped wagons which were moved along by horses concealed inside; there were also marksmen hidden inside the wagons. These war-engines can be included among the main forerunners of the modern tank.

The indefatigable mounts ridden by the Russian cavalry were the *zemaïtuka* (a cross between the wild horse of Mongolia and the Arab), the *bashkir* (a breed found in the steppes or in mountain regions), and the *kazak*, which could sometimes be seen marching at an ambling pace. These horses measured, on average, 1.30 metres in height at the withers. They seldom required shoeing and could live on practically nothing, yet were capable of making journeys of up to 300 kilometres a day.

The method used to break in these wild horses consisted of galloping the captured animal until it dropped from sheer exhaustion. It was then immediately tightly bound and its ears and nostrils tied with a fine cord. Thus it was sheer pain that made the animal tractable. However, such was the energy of these horses[1] that two out of ten of them proved untameable, even after this harsh treatment.[2]

---

[1] They were probably tarpans, a particularly intractable, aggressive, and stubborn breed which became extinct at the end of the 18th century.

[2] This treatment was still in use at the beginning of the previous century in the Ukraine, and was probably very widespread in Russia among primitive peoples. Russian war-horses were usually geldings, that is, horses that had been castrated. This ancient custom made the animal gentler in nature.

CHINA AND JAPAN IN THE 16TH CENTURY

1. Chinese soldier from the crack division known as the Tigers. The buckler he is carrying, known as a *ton-pey*, is made out of reeds wound round in a spiral pattern. 2. Standard-bearer of a platoon of Chinese crossbowmen; note his repeater bow with its loading lever which could fire eight to ten arrows in rapid succession. 3. Archer of the Imperial Chinese Guard. 4. Samurai warrior (early 16th century). His helmet, called a *mempo*, has a half-mask attached to it; it is decorated with the *kuwagata*, an ornamental pattern representing the stylized leaves of an aquatic plant. He is wearing lamellar armour in the *do-maru* style (meaning literally, 'round the body'). The sabres hanging at his belt are collectively called *daisho*. 5. Samurai warrior wearing *tosei-gusoki* armour, a kind of one-piece cuirass (second half of the 16th century). (See fig 8). 6. *Mempo* helmet with a half-mask (16th century). The nose-piece is detachable. 7. *So-men* helmet with a full mask (16th century). 8. *So-men* helmet (16th century). It belongs to the suit of armour shown in fig. 5.

1

6

7

2

3

4

8

5

Tartars and Mongols

The name Tartar, or more accurately, Tatar, was originally used to describe a Mongol tribe at the time of Genghis Khan; however, from the 13th century onwards it was applied to a succession of Turkish tribes.

Among the authentic Tartar tribes were the Nogais of the Crimea, who only became a tributary of Russia in 1783. They were great horsemen – the equivalent of pirates in the steppes – and they were extraordinarily skilful at covering their tracks. When the Nogais went on a raid, they would travel in a body of 400 riders until they were about 80 kilometres from their chosen target. They would then split up into four groups of 100 men, each of which would travel in the direction of one of the four points of the compass. After covering a distance of 5 kilometres each band of 100 men divided into three groups; one of these would continue advancing straight ahead, while the two remaining groups chose routes at right angles to that of the first group. Three kilometres further on each group would split up once more into three divisions which travelled away from one another in a three-pronged formation for a distance of 1 kilometre. All these operations were carried out with the aid of a primitive compass; this valuable instrument then helped the 400 marauders, who were now scattered to the four points of the compass, to make the final ride that would enable them to join up again at the point agreed on beforehand near the village they were planning to strike. The tremendous value of all these manoeuvres was that they frustrated the attempts of even the most skilful Cossack to track them through the grass of the steppes; the diverging trails would increase and multiply in all directions, until eventually the final squads of riders were leaving a maze of thirty-six barely visible tracks behind them.

Under Turkish rule the Tartars were organized into units known as *kazans* (meaning 'pots' – soldiers in a group all ate from the same cooking-pot). Each kazan was led by a *mirza* who was appointed by the khan, who was himself a subject of the Sultan. The Nogais carried on a lucrative trade in slaves, selling them in lots of 30,000 at a time in the markets of Sinope, Trebizond, and Constantinople.

When the Tartars were driven back by weight of numbers (they usually only agreed to fight when they outnumbered the enemy by ten to one) they would draw themselves up in a semi-circle formation, charge, then suddenly scatter in all directions, releasing a hail of arrows behind them. The Poles called this tactic 'the dance of the Tartars'.

We should also say something about the Mongols, those famous conquerors whose empire was founded in 1206 by Gengis Khan, re-established by Tamburlaine in 1369, and restored again by Baber in 1505.

The basic unit of the Mongol army was the *arban* (a platoon of ten men). Ten *arbans* made up a *djaghoum* (a squadron), ten squadrons formed a *minggam* (a regiment) and ten regiments made a *tumen*, or a division of 10,000 men. Their tactics relied on speed, cunning, and the terror inspired by the threat of certain death.

The Turks

The period of Turkish military supremacy falls between 1300 and 1550.[1] The army was chiefly made up of mercenary troops (often European in origin), irregular footsoldiers known as *bashi-bazouks* (meaning 'without a head or leader'), and mounted soldiers called *akibis*. The mounted *sipahis* (*spahis*) and janissaries were the élite corps of the sultan.

ORIENTALS (i)

1 and 2. Turkish *provocateurs* known as *deli*. They acted as heralds and carried challenges and summons from the Sultan to the enemy. 3. Officer of the *carpici*, who were scouts in the Janissary cavalry. 4. Regular Turkish cavalryman or *alkans* carrying a standard with the sabre of Allah; this was a sacred emblem for all Turks. Although the colour traditionally associated with the prophet was green, Turkish standards and flags were to be found in large numbers and in a wide variety of colours. In addition to these there were the *thougs*, or horses' tails, which served to indicate the rank of military leaders (see fig. 1). 5. Turkish volunteer cavalryman. 6. Spahis in the Janissary cavalry. 7. Persian soldier (16th century). He is wearing body-armour made in four pieces called *char-aïna* (literally, 'four mirrors'). His distinctive *kulah-khud* helmet and armour were worn for several centuries. 8. Spanish Moor (15th century). He is armed with a Moroccan *nimcha*.

[1] The prayer known as the angelus originally recommended to God those Christians fighting against Mohammed II in the 15th century.

The janissaries reached their maximum strength, around 15,000 men, in the 16th century.

The basic fighting unit was the *orta*, which at various times numbered anything from 100 to 3,000 men. One of the traditional insignia of the janissaries was a wooden spoon that fitted in the plume-tube of the hat. Each rank corresponded to a culinary function. The company commander was 'master chef', and the first officer was 'master of the soup tureen'. The sultan was known as 'the father who provided'.

The cooking-pot, or *kazan*, was the emblem of the *orta*. Allowing it to be captured meant disgrace, while turning it upside down signified rebellion.[1]

The cavalry, which constituted by far the largest section of the army, had at its disposal in 1520 ten to twelve thousand horses. Each *sipahi* had a retinue of two to six horsemen, following the example of the European 'lance'.

The Turkish artillery, which was introduced in 1364, was truly formidable. Several references are made to it throughout the three volumes of this work.

The superb horses used by the Turkish cavalry were of a variety of different breeds. The Arab half-blood from the Caspian region could travel 800 kilometres in six days. The Arab horses best suited for warfare came from Kurdistan and Persia. A more heavily built type of horse, called a turkoman, was also used in battle. The finest Arab thorough-breds were reared in the Hedjaz, while the sturdiest Arab horses came from the Yemen. The most graceful gait belonged to the thoroughbreds of the Negev region, and the liveliest Arabian horses came from Egypt. The finest coats were found on Syrian thoroughbreds.

A final word here concerning the sacred banner of the Prophet. It was made from 4 metres of green silk, and its pole had a gold clenched fist on the end holding a book or the Koran written in the hand of Caliph Omar, the second successor to Mohammed. Any Christian whose gaze defiled it was put to death instantly.

---

[1] The creation of the modern Turkish army in 1826 led to the cooking pot being overturned – and the janissaries being completely massacred.

China

Chinese armies were dominated for a long time by the Tartar troops of Manchuria, which at that time were the only fighters to really qualify for the name of soldier.

The practice of distinguishing troop corps by means of different-coloured flags seems to date back to earliest times. In the course of our research into the subject we have come up with some odd items of information which are difficult to arrange in any kind of strict chronological order.

The colours of the élite Manchurian troops were yellow, those of the Mongol army white, and those of the Chinese red; mercenaries and prisoners of war flew a green flag. Later we find élite Tartar troops flying yellow, white, red, and blue standards, while the green standard was used by the Chinese. The troops' jackets were the same colour as their standard. One final distribution of colours which we have come across goes as follows: yellow, cavalry; white, archers and arbalesters; green, pikemen; blue, rondachiers; red, arquebusiers; and black, artillerymen.

The nine ranks of officers were distinguished by a ball worn on top of the head. In order of rank the balls went as follows: red, light blue, dark blue, crystal, white stone, and gold. Variations on these were used to differentiate the three remaining lower ranks. The hierarchy of officers was distinguished by pectorals decorated with animals, dragons, lions, unicorns, and other animals.

The weapons and equipment used by the Chinese appear to have remained unchanged for several

ORIENTALS (ii)

1. *Onbachi* or corporal. The ornamental tube on his headdress was for holding the regimental soup-ladle. 2. Turkish artillery-man or *jopegs*. 3. Lieutenant or *karakoulloutchi*. His headdress is decorated with the highly-coveted 'great palm of courage'. 4. Archer of the Guard or *solachi*. 5. Janissary private. 6. Mounted janissary or *ulufage*. 7. Captain of the bodyguard, or *noundji*. 8. The agha, or supreme leader of the Janissaries. The turban only grew to these proportions after the capture of Constantinople in 1453. 9. Captain or *bolucbassa* carrying the great ladle; after the cooking pot, this was the most sacred emblem of the Janissaries. Any man who was condemned to death but who managed to touch it was instantly reprieved. All the soldiers shown in this plate are Janissaries, except for fig. 2.

centuries. From the 4th century onwards élite warriors wore a kind of kaftan known as a *kwei-kya* that was probably of Mongol origin; it had shoulder pieces crudely armoured with metal plaquettes or laquered leather.

Although the Chinese knew about bombs and incendiary rockets several centuries before Europe, they did not use firearms until the 18th century, and as late as the middle of the last century they still preferred to use the bow and crossbow.

Japan

The lack of development in weapons is even more striking in the case of Japan. A perfect illustration of this is the firearm, which was introduced into the country by the Dutch and Portuguese.

The matchlock arquebus, which was introduced into Japan at the beginning of the 16th century, developed into a weapon with a slightly curved butt and a finely decorated barrel, more in keeping with the traditional Japanese simplicity and purity of line. As a result of allowing foreigners back into the country in 1860, the Japanese adopted the fulminate percussion rifle – thereby catching up, in one leap, over 200 years of development of a weapon which had made no progress in their own country.

Japanese armour was far less resistant than European versions, and it underwent its only real phase of development in the 16th century, when Europeans wearing light cuirasses appeared on the scene. The samurais were very impressed by the smooth body armour of the Europeans and adopted their own version of the 'one-piece cuirass', the *tosei gusoki*, and, later on, the small plates on the arm and forearm, known in Japanese as *o-tataage no suneate*.

The oldest and most classic type of armour, the *do-maru*, was made entirely out of rows of plaques arranged in sets of seven by a complicated and highly elaborate method of silk lacing. The *do-maru* goes at least as far back as the 13th century, and was probably worn by the original samurais in the 10th and 11th centuries. The small plates, made of metal, leather and even cardboard, were lacquered in every imaginable shade and colour and were sometimes inlaid with gold or fully gilded. The primitive beauty of these suits of Japanese armour makes them a star attraction in many museums today.[1]

[1] They are usually light in comparison to European suits of armour. We owned a *tosei gusoki* suit which weighed barely 5 kilos, including the helmet.

The masked helmet was only introduced in Japan, in our opinion, as a direct result of the influence of the first Europeans; the same can be said for the cabasset-type helmet worn there, the bullet-proof *bachi*. The ornamental horns known as *kuwagata* that appeared on helmets were originally more slender and tapering in shape. They appear to have been reserved exclusively for outstanding warriors in the cavalry.

The infantry wore identical helmets and cuirasses, though in the 13th century they went barelegged and barefoot. However, there are examples of them shown wearing only body armour and greaves, with baggy sleeves and trousers and a conical-shaped hat of black felt. Later on sandals and shoes of bearskin were introduced, as were sheaths made, like the horses' shabracks, out of bear- or panther-skin. All of which added a colourful and primitive note to the striking appearance of these formidable warriors.

The most ruthless cruelty was commonplace in the Japanese armies: one tradition consisted of threading enemies' heads on long sabres like a grisly string of beads. We should hastily point out here that this horrible custom was just as eagerly practised in Europe well into the 16th century: at the time of the Renaissance, collars made of human remains were sometimes used to adorn the soldiery of our so-called 'civilized' continent.

The weapons traditionally used by all warriors, from the humblest class, the *kumebe*, to the samurais themselves were a bow 2.20 metres long with an outside grip, which was succeeded by the laminated bow of Asia. The *katana* sabre, worn in conjunction with the *tachi* sabre, made up the *daisho*, or traditional weapons of the samurai warrior. The *katana* was worn with its blade facing downwards, while the *tachi* faced in the opposite direction. All the other types of sabre, like the *sho-to* and *wakizashi* were, like those already mentioned, of extraordinarily high quality and temper. They were capable of slicing through large nails, copper ingots, and, of course, the body of a human being, without being blunted.

The Japanese horse, which was very small, had been imported into the country in the third century. It was shod with thonged sandals instead of metal horseshoes. Occasionally it wore a caparison of ring mail in the 16th and 17th centuries. The wooden spurs and saddles used by the Japanese mounted soldier were very light and magnificently worked, as was the rest of Japanese military equipment.

Index